Titanic & Lusitania

Survivor Stories

From the Best of Times To The Worst of Times
based on the Logan Marshall classics

Edited by Bruce M. Caplan
and Ken Rossignol

Seattle Miracle Inc.
comic@aol.com ken.thechesapeake@gmail.com
www.SinkingTitanic.com
www.privateerclause.com

ISBN: 094461099
ISBN-13: 978-0964461093

DEDICATION

We dedicate this narrative to the great reporting of Logan Marshall---

To all those who perished on the *Titanic* and the *Lusitania.*

And to General Pershing and the American Soldiers who fought with such distinction in World War I.

CONTENTS

TITANIC & LUSITANIA

Introduction

In 1953 the wonderful movie *Titanic* staring Clifton Webb and Barbara Stanwyk was released to the public. My 5th grade teacher was mesmerized by the feature and she was able to persuade me to become a life-long *Titanic* Buff. In the years since, I've devoured scores of books about the tragedy and watched every video that I could get my hands on.

The most influential narrative that I read was Walter Lord's *A Night to Remember*. His book came out in 1955 and described in great detail what happened on the fatal night and morning of April 14-15 1912.

In 1981 my secretary Mary Ambur gave me a gift of the first book that was published after the demise of the Titanic. The name of the tome *was The Sinking of the Titanic and Great Sea Disasters*. The author was Logan Marshall a noted journalist and author of many true narratives.

The pages were tattered and worn, but the information was mind boggling! On page 31 of the book it said... "Unknown to the passengers the *Titanic* was on fire from the day she set sail from Southampton....."

It was 1981 and the *Titanic* had not yet been discovered. Whenever I discussed Marshall's text with my associates I was told that it was dubious whether the

Titanic was on fire and surely if it was true it would have been mentioned in other texts about the *Titanic.*

As the years passed I began to believe that Logan Marshall as an investigative journalist had uncovered a giant secret about the *Titanic.* I was almost certain that when the passengers boarded the ship one of the coal bins was a fire and that fire could have been one of the major causes of the demise of the great ship

As I read Marshall's text I soon realized that he had very valuable information from primary sources but in his haste to get his book out he had not had time to edit it properly. In 1995, I took on the task of re-editing his great narrative.

I soon realized that I and the rest of the public were only interested in the saga of the *Titanic* and not the other Sea Disasters. My editing took a couple of months and I tried to improve on the unity, and transition of his work.

In editing the text I consulted my uncle Theodore Kaplan. He had worked in the shipyards during World War II and was somewhat of an expert on the forensics of steel. He told me that if the ship was on fire for several days in the same location or near the location where it encountered the iceberg---the fire would have weakened the Titanic.

His conclusion was ... "The Titanic would probably have survived the crash with the iceberg had it not been for the fire." He felt that the only reason that the iceberg was able to do so much damage was because the coal fire had taken the strength out of much of the metal.

My edited edition of Marshall's text came out in October of 1996. I was not the first in the modern era to mention the coal fire but I do believe that I was the first to hypothesize that the coal fire was a significant source of the demise of the great ship?

Marshall's ability to be a time machine and catapult us back to 1912 was amazing. He went on to write many more wonderful true narratives.

In January 2011, I was invited to be a guest speaker on the *Celebrity Mercury* cruise ship. My topic was the Titanic along with other nautical subjects. I did three back to back cruises on the Mercury from Baltimore to the Caribbean. For this wonderful adventure I want to thank Carol and Elayne at Posh Talks.

On my second day at sea I gave my first lecture. I always begin by pointing out that if the Titanic had just had enough lifeboats everyone would have been saved. My first speech is titled---"The Sinking of the Titanic" and why the lessons made cruising so safe today!"

I always meet the most fantastic people on cruise ships. The *Mercury* was no exception. There was Al Goldis who lectured about baseball. He had worked for Gene Autry for almost a decade. Then there was Richard Rubin who can play a piano and make you laugh better than anyone I've ever experienced!

At brunch that day my wife Esther and I were seated with a couple from Maryland. Donna and Ken Rossignol and I learned he was a journalist from Maryland.

Ken and I both love to talk and write and soon he and his wife Donna were joining me and my wife Esther for breakfast each morning. Ken had already written several great books in the fiction genre. I told him that someday it would be great if we could collaborate on a true narrative.

Since that time, Ken has written two wonderful nonfiction gems----The Story of the Rag about operating his newspaper in Maryland for over 22 years and his most recent publication *Titanic 1912* where he brought back the original newspaper accounts from 1912 and analyzed them. His series of cruise thrillers has now grown to four books: *The Privateer Clause, Return of the Sea Empress, Follow Titanic and Follow Triangle-Vanish*. He has also published two collections of short stories from his monthly publication *The Chesapeake*.

We decided that our first cooperative effort would be to bring back to the public in edited form more of the wonderful Logan Marshall information from long ago.

In the following Marshall selections you'll discover the facts about the *RMS Titanic* and her demise. Then through Logan Marshall's writings we'll see the elements of what caused The Great War or as it's labeled today---World War I, to break out. We'll then review the demise of the *Lusitania* with Marshall's fantastic interviews and information.

In this narrative we begin when the world is at total peace. People that board the *Titanic* are all smiling. After the *Titanic* the world slides into bitter struggles and only someone like Logan Marshall who had the unique ability to report the facts can take you on this educational journey. Ken and I hope that you enjoy your literary voyage back to yesterday!

Most Sincerely,

Bruce M. Caplan and Ken Rossignol

THE SPHERE

AN ILLUSTRATED NEWSPAPER FOR THE HOME

With which is incorporated "BLACK & WHITE"

Volume XLIX. No. 639. London, April 20, 1912. [WITH SUPPLEMENT] Price Sixpence.

THE GREATEST WRECK IN THE WORLD'S MARITIME HISTORY—THE LOSS OF THE "TITANIC"

The above composite picture is given not as an actual document but as some realisation of essential factors in the loss of the great White Star liner. Seeing that she sank at 2.20 a.m. on Sunday night no actual records of the vessel's meeting with the ice are likely to be forthcoming. The icebergs shown here are reproduced from photographs obtained off Newfoundland. The size of them of course varies very considerably according to the season. The height of the vessel's bow above water-line would be about 60 ft. The opening shown near the top was a cable socket for a bow hawser, used when entering harbours.

CHAPTER I

The Titanic Facts

THE statistical record of the great ship has news value at this time. Early in 1908 officials of the White Star Company announced that they would eclipse all previous records in shipbuilding with a vessel of staggering dimensions. The result was the *RMS Titanic*. The keel of the ill-fated ship was laid in the summer of 1909 at the Harland & Wolff yards, Belfast. Lord Pierre, considered one of the best authorities on shipbuilding in the world, was the designer. The leviathan was launched on May 31, 1911, and was completed in February, 1912, at a cost of $10,000,000.

SISTER SHIP OF *OLYMPIC*

The *Titanic,* largest liner in commission, was a sister ship of the *Olympic*. The registered tonnage of each vessel is estimated as 45,000, but officers of the White Star Line say that the *Titanic* measured 46,328 tons. The *Titanic* was commanded by Captain E. J. Smith, the White Star admiral, who had previously been on the *Olympic*.

She was 882 1/2 long, or about four city blocks, and was 5000 tons bigger than a battleship twice as large as the dreadnought *USS Delaware*. Like her sister ship, the *Olympic*, the *Titanic* was a four-funneled vessel, and had eleven decks. The distance from the keel to the top of the funnels was 175 feet. She had an average speed of twenty-one knots.

The *Titanic* could accommodate 2500 passengers. The steamship was divided into numerous compartments, separated by fifteen bulkheads. She was equipped with a gymnasium, swimming pool, hospital with operating room, and a grill and palm garden.

CARRIED CREW OF 860

The registered tonnage was 46,328, and the displacement tonnage 66,000. She was capable of carrying 2500 passengers and the crew numbered 860.

The largest plates employed in the hull were 36 feet long, weighing 43 1/2 tons each, and the largest steel beam used was 92 feet long, the weight of this double beam being 4 tons. The rudder, which was operated electrically, weighed 100 tons, the anchors 15 1/2 tons each, the center (turbine) propeller 22 tons, and each of the two "wing" propellers 38 tons each.

The after "boss-arms," from which were suspended the three propeller shafts, tipped the scales at 73 1/2 tons, and the forward "boss-arms" at 45 tons. Each link in the anchor-chains weighed 175 pounds. There were more than 2000 side-lights and windows to light the public rooms and passenger cabins.

Nothing was left to chance in the construction of the *Titanic*. Three million rivets (weighing 1200 tons) held the solid plates of steel together. To insure stability in binding the heavy plates in the double bottom, half a million rivets, weighing about 270 tons, were used. All the plating of the hulls was riveted by hydraulic power, driving seven-ton riveting machines, suspended from traveling cranes. The double bottom extended the full length of the vessel, varying from 5 feet 3 inches to 6 feet 3 inches in depth, and lent added strength to the hull.

MOST LUXURIOUS STEAMSHIP

Not only was the *Titanic* the largest steamship afloat but it was the most luxurious. Elaborately furnished cabins opened onto her eleven decks, and some of these decks were reserved as private promenades that were engaged with the best suites. One of these suites was sold for $4,350 for the boat's maiden and only voyage. Suites similar, but which were without the private promenade decks, sold for $2,300.

The Titanic differed in some respects from her sister ship. The *Olympic* has a lower promenade deck, but in the *Titanic's* case the staterooms were brought out flush with the outside of the superstructure, and the rooms themselves made much larger. The sitting rooms of some of the suites on this deck were 15 x 15 feet.

The restaurant was much larger than that of the *Olympic* and it had a novelty in the shape of a private promenade deck on the starboard side, to be used exclusively by its patrons. Adjoining it was a reception room, where hosts and hostesses could meet their guests. Two private promenades were connected with the two most luxurious suites on the ship. The suites were situated about amidships; one on either side of the vessel, and each was about fifty feet long. One of the suites comprised a sitting room, two bedrooms and a bath.

These private promenades were expensive luxuries. The cost figured out something like forty dollars a front foot for a six days' voyage. They, with the suites to which they are attached, were the most expensive transatlantic accommodations yet offered.

THE ENGINE ROOM

The engine room was divided into two sections, one given to the reciprocating engines and the other to the turbines. There were two sets of the reciprocating kind, one working each of the wing propellers through a four-cylinder triple expansion, direct acting inverted engine. Each set could generate 15,000 indicated horsepower at seventy-five revolutions a minute. The Parsons turbine takes steam from the reciprocating engines, and by developing a horse-power of 16,000 at 165 revolutions a minute works the third of the ship's propellers, the one directly under the rudder. Of the four funnels of the vessel three were connected with the engine room and the fourth or after funnel for ventilating the ship including the gallery.

Practically all of the space on the *Titanic* below the upper deck was occupied by steam-generating plant, coal bunkers and propelling machinery. Eight of the fifteen water-tight compartments contained the mechanical part of the vessel. There were, for instance, twenty-four double end and five single end boilers, each 16 feet 9 inches in diameter, the larger 20 feet long and the smaller 11 feet 9 inches long. The larger boilers had six fires under each of them and the smaller three furnaces. Coal was stored in bunker space along the side of the ship between the lower and middle decks, and was first shipped from there into bunkers running all the way across the vessel in the lowest part. From there the stokers handed it into the furnaces.

One of the most interesting features of the vessel was the refrigerating plant, which comprised a huge ice-making and refrigerating machine and a number of provision rooms on the after part of the lower decks. There were separate cold rooms for beef, mutton, poultry, game, fish, vegetables, fruit, butter, bacon, cheese, flowers, mineral water, wine, spirits and champagne, all maintained at different temperatures most suitable to each. Perishable freight had a compartment of its own, also chilled by the plant.

COMFORT AND STABILITY

Two main ideas were carried out in the *Titanic.* One was comfort and the other stability. The vessel was planned to be an ocean ferry. She was to have only a speed of twenty-one knots, far below that of some other modern vessels, but she was planned to make that speed, blow high or blow low, so that if she left one side of the ocean at a given time she could be relied on to reach the other side at almost a certain minute of a certain hour. One who has looked into modern methods for safe guarding a vessel of the *Titanic* type can hardly imagine an accident that could cause her to founder. No collision such as has been the fate of any ship in recent years, it has been thought up to this time, could send her down, nor could running against an iceberg do it unless such an accident were coupled with the remotely possible blowing out of a boiler.

She would sink at once, probably, if she were to run over a submerged rock or derelict in such manner that both her keel plates and her double bottom were torn away for more than half her length; but such a catastrophe was so remotely possible that it did not even enter the field of conjecture. The reason for all this is found in the modern arrangement of water-tight steel compartments into which all ships now are divided and of which the *Titanic* had fifteen so disposed that half of them, including the largest, could be flooded without impairing the safety of the vessel. Probably it was the working of these bulkheads and the water-tight doors between them as they are supposed to work that saved the *Titanic* from foundering when she struck the iceberg.

These bulkheads were of heavy sheet steel and started at the very bottom of the ship and extended right up to the top side. The openings in the bulkheads were just about the size of the ordinary doorway, but the doors did not swing as in a house, but fitted into water-tight grooves above the opening. They could be released instantly in several ways, and once closed formed a barrier to the water as solid as the bulkhead itself.

In the *Titanic*, as in other great modern ships, these doors were held in place above the openings by friction clutches. On the bridge was a switch which connected with an electric magnet at the side of the bulkhead opening. The turning of this switch caused the magnet to draw down a heavy weight, which instantly released the friction clutch, and allowed the door to fall or slide down over the opening in a second. If, however, through accident the bridge switch was rendered useless the doors would close automatically in a few seconds. This was arranged by means of large metal floats at the side of the doorways, which rested just above the level of the double bottom, and as the water entered the compartments these floats would rise to it and directly release the clutch holding the door open. These clutches could also be released by hand.

It was said of the *Titanic* that liner compartments could be flooded as far back or as far forward as the engine room and she would float, though she might take on a heavy list, or settle considerably at one end. To provide against just such an accident as she is said to have encountered she had set back a good distance from the bows an extra heavy cross partition known as the collision bulkhead, which would prevent water getting in amidships, even though a good part of her bow should be torn away.

What a ship can stand and still float was shown a few years ago when the *Suevic* of the White Star Line went on the rocks on the British coast. The wreckers could not move the forward part of her, so they separated her into two sections by the use of dynamite, and after putting in a temporary bulkhead floated off the after half of the ship, put it in dry dock and built a new forward part for her. More recently the battleship *Maine* or what was left of her, was floated out to sea, and kept on top of the water by her water-tight compartments only.

The Olympic and the Titanic shown being constructed side by side at Harland & Wolff shipyard in Belfast

48 *THE SPHERE*

THE GREATEST SHIPWRECK IN THE WORLD'S

THE SUMPTUOUS APPOINTMENTS OF THE "TITANIC"—THE PARISIAN CAFE WITH ITS TRELLISWORK AND CLIMBING PLANTS

A Sitting-room of a Private Suite on the "Titanic"

Cycle Racing Machine in the Gymnasium

HOW THE WHITE STAR LINER "TITANIC" ENCOUNTERED

CHAPTER II
THE MAIDEN VOYAGE OF THE TITANIC

NEVER was an ill-starred voyage more auspiciously begun than when the *Titanic,* newly crowned empress of the seas, steamed majestically out of the port of Southampton at noon on Wednesday, April 10th, bound for New York. Elaborate preparations had been made for the maiden voyage. Crowds of eager watchers gathered to witness the departure, all the more interested because of the notable people who were to travel aboard her. Friends and relatives of many of the passengers were at the dock to bid Godspeed to their departing loved ones. The passengers themselves were unusually gay and happy.

Majestic and beautiful the ship rested on the water, a marvel of shipbuilding, worthy of any sea. As this new queen of the ocean moved slowly from her dock, no one questioned her construction: she was fitted with an elaborate system of water-tight compartments, calculated to make her unsinkable; she had been pronounced the safest as well as the most sumptuous Atlantic liner afloat.

There was silence just before the boat pulled out—the silence that usually precedes the leave-taking. The heavy whistles sounded and the splendid *Titanic*, her flags flying and her band playing, churned the water and plowed heavily away.

Then the *Titanic*, with the people on board waving handkerchiefs and shouting good-byes that could be heard only as a buzzing murmur on shore, rode away on the ocean, proudly, majestically, her head up and, so it seemed, her shoulders thrown back. If ever a vessel seemed to throb with proud life, if ever a monster of the sea seemed to "feel its oats" and strain at the leash, if ever a ship seemed to have breeding and blue blood that would keep it going until its heart broke, that ship was the *Titanic*.

And so it was only her due that as the *Titanic* steamed out of the harbor bound on her maiden voyage a thousand "God-speeds" were wafted after her, while every other vessel that she passed, the greatest of them dwarfed by her colossal proportions, paid homage to the new queen regnant with the blasts of their whistles and the shrieking of steam sirens.

THE SHIP'S CAPTAIN

In command of the *Titanic* was Captain E. J. Smith, a veteran of the seas, and admiral of the White Star Line fleet. The next six officers, in the order of their rank, were Murdock, Lightoller, Pitman, Boxhall, Lowe and Moody. Jack Phillips was chief wireless operator, with Harold Bride as assistant.

From the forward bridge, fully ninety feet above the sea, peered out the benign face of the ship's master, cool of aspect, deliberate of action, impressive in that quality of confidence that is bred only of long experience in command.

From far below the bridge sounded the strains of the ship's orchestra, playing blithely a favorite air from "The Chocolate Soldier." All went as merry as a wedding bell. Indeed, among that gay ship's company were two score or more at least for whom the wedding bells had sounded in truth not many days before. Some were on their honeymoon tours, others were returning to their motherland after having passed the weeks of the honeymoon, like Colonel John Jacob Astor and his young bride, amid the diversions of Egypt or other Old World countries.

What daring flight of imagination would have ventured the prediction that within the span of six days that stately ship, humbled, shattered and torn asunder, would lie two thousand fathoms deep at the bottom of the Atlantic, that the benign face that peered from the bridge would be set in the rigor of death and that the happy bevy of voyaging brides would be sorrowing widows?

ALMOST IN A COLLISION

The big vessel had, however, a touch of evil fortune before she cleared the harbor of Southampton. As she passed down stream her immense bulk—she displaced 66,000 tons—drew the waters after her with an irresistible suction that tore the American liner *New York* from her moorings; seven steel hawsers were snapped like twine. *The New York* floated toward the White Star ship, and would have rammed the new ship had not the tugs Vulcan and Neptune stopped her and towed her back to the quay.

When the mammoth ship touched at Cherbourg and later at Queenstown she was again the object of a port ovation, the smaller craft doing obeisance while thousands gazed in wonder at her stupendous proportions. After taking aboard some additional passengers at each port, the *Titanic* headed her towering bow toward the open sea and the race for a record on her maiden voyage was begun.

NEW BURST OF SPEED EACH DAY

The *Titanic* made 484 miles as her first day's run, her powerful new engines turning over at the rate of seventy revolutions. On the second day out the speed was hit up to seventy-three revolutions and the run for the day was bulletined as 519 miles. Still further increasing the speed, the rate of revolution of the engines was raised to seventy-five and the day's run was 549 miles, the best yet scheduled.

But the ship had not yet been speeded to her capacity she was capable of turning over about seventy-eight revolutions. Had the weather conditions been favorable, it was intended to press the great racer to the full limit of her speed on Monday. But for the *Titanic* Monday never came.

FIRE IN THE COAL BUNKERS

Unknown to the passengers, the *Titanic* was on fire from the day she sailed from Southampton. Her officers and crew knew it, for they had fought the fire for days. This story, told for the first time by the survivors of the crew, was only one of the many thrilling tales of the fateful first voyage.

"The *Titanic* sailed from Southampton on Wednesday, April 10th, at noon," said J. Dilley, fireman on the *Titanic*. "I was assigned to the *Titanic* from the *Oceanic*, where I had served as a fireman. From the day we sailed the *Titanic* was on fire, and my sole duty, together with eleven other men, had been to fight that fire. We had made no headway against it."

PASSENGERS IN IGNORANCE

"Of course," he went on, "the passengers knew nothing of the fire. Do you think we'd have let them know about it? No, sir.

"The fire started in bunker No. 6. There were hundreds of tons of coal stored there. The coal on top of the bunker was wet, as all the coal should have been, but down at the bottom of the bunker the coal had been permitted to get dry. "The dry coal at the bottom of the pile took fire, and smoldered for days. The wet coal on top kept the flames from coming through, but down in the bottom of the bunkers the flames were raging. "Two men from each watch of stokers were tolled off, to fight that fire. The stokers worked four hours at a time, so twelve of us were fighting flames from the day we put out of Southampton until we hit the iceberg.

"No, we didn't get that fire out, and among the stokers there was talk that we'd have to empty the big coal bunkers after we'd put our passengers off in New York, and then call on the fire-boats there to help us put out the fire. "The stokers were alarmed over it, but the officers told us to keep our mouths shut—they didn't want to alarm the passengers."

USUAL DIVERSION

Until Sunday, April 14th, the voyage had apparently been a delightful but uneventful one. The passengers had passed the time in the usual diversions of ocean travelers, amusing themselves in the luxurious saloons, promenading on the boat deck, lolling at their ease in steamer chairs and making pools on the daily runs of the steamship. The smoking rooms and card rooms had been as well patronized as usual, and a party of several notorious professional gamblers had begun reaping their usual easy harvest.

As early as Sunday afternoon the officers of the *Titanic* must have known that they were approaching dangerous ice fields of the kind that are a perennial menace to the safety of steamships following the regular transatlantic lanes off the Great Banks of Newfoundland.

AN UNHEEDED WARNING

On Sunday afternoon the *Titanic*'s wireless operator forwarded to the Hydrographic office in Washington, Baltimore, Philadelphia and elsewhere the following dispatch: "April 14.—The German steamship *Amerika* (Hamburg-American Line) reports by radio-telegraph passing two large icebergs in latitude 41.27, longitude 50.08.—Titanic, Br. S. S."

Despite this warning, the *Titanic* forged ahead Sunday night at her usual speed—from twenty-one to twenty-five knots.

The mighty propellers of the Titanic loom over workers.

The Titanic prepares to leave on its first and only voyage.

CHAPTER III

THE TITANIC STRIKES AN ICEBERG!

SUNDAY night the magnificent ocean liner was plunging through a comparatively placid sea, on the surface of which there was much mushy ice and here and there a number of comparatively harmless-looking floes. The night was clear and stars visible. First Officer William T. Murdock was in charge of the bridge. The first suggestion of the presence of the iceberg that he received was from the lookout in the crow's nest.

Three warnings were transmitted from the crow's nest of the Titanic to the officer on the doomed steamship's bridge 15 minutes before she struck, according to Thomas Whiteley, a first saloon steward. Whiteley, who was whipped overboard from the ship by a rope while helping to lower a life-boat, finally reported on the Carpathia aboard one of the boats that contained, he said, both the crow's nest lookouts.

He heard a conversation between them, he asserted, in which they discussed the warnings given to the *Titanic*'s bridge of the presence of the iceberg.

Whiteley did not know the names of either of the lookout men and believed that they returned to England with the majority of the surviving members of the crew.

"I heard one of them say that at 11:15, 15 minutes before the Titanic struck, he had reported to First Officer Murdock, on the bridge, that he fancied he saw an iceberg!" said Whiteley. "Twice after that, the lookout said, he warned Murdock that a berg was ahead. They were very indignant that no attention was paid to their warnings."

TARDY ATTENTION TO WARNING RESPONSIBLE FOR ACCIDENT

Murdock's tardy answering of a telephone call from the crow's nest is assigned by Whiteley as the cause of the disaster. When Murdock answered the call he received the information that the iceberg was due ahead. This information was imparted just a few seconds before the crash, and had the officer promptly answered the ring of the bell it is probable that the accident could have been avoided, or at least, been reduced by the lowered speed.

The lookout saw a towering "blue berg" looming up in the sea path of the *Titanic*, and called the bridge on the ship's telephone. When, after the passing of those two or three fateful minutes an officer on the bridge lifted the telephone receiver from its hook to answer the lookout, it was too late.

The speeding liner, cleaving a calm sea under a star-studded sky, had reached the floating mountain of ice, which the theoretically "unsinkable" ship struck a crashing, if glancing, blow with her starboard bow.

VAIN TRY TO CLEAR BERG

The first officer did what other startled and alert commanders would have done under similar circumstances, that is he made an effort by going full speed ahead on the starboard propeller and reversing his port propeller, simultaneously throwing his helm over, to make a rapid turn and clear the berg. The maneuver was not successful.

He succeeded in saving his bows from crashing into the ice-cliff, but nearly the entire length of the underbody of the great ship on the starboard side was ripped. The speed of the *Titanic*, estimated to be at least twenty-one knots, was so terrific that the knife-like edge of the iceberg's spur protruding under the sea cut through her like a can-opener.

The *Titanic* was in 41.46 north latitude and 50.14 west longitudes when she was struck, very near the spot on the wide Atlantic where the *Carmania* encountered a field of ice, studded with great bergs, on her voyage to New York which ended on April 14th. It was really an ice pack, due to an unusually severe winter in the north Atlantic. No less than twenty-five bergs, some of great height, were counted.

The shock was almost imperceptible. The first officer did not apparently realize that the great ship had received her death wound, and none of the passengers had the slightest suspicion that anything more than a usual minor sea accident had happened. Hundreds who had gone to their berths and were asleep were unawakened by the vibration.

BRIDGE GAME NOT DISTURBED

To illustrate the placidity with which practically all the men regarded the accident it is related that Pierre Marechal, son of the vice-admiral of the French navy, Lucien Smith, Paul Chevre, a French sculptor, and A. F. Ormont, a cotton broker, were in the Cafe Parisien playing bridge.

The four calmly got up from the table and after walking on deck and looking over the rail returned to their game. One of them had left his cigar on the card table, and while the three others were gazing out on the sea he remarked that he couldn't afford to lose his smoke, returned for his cigar and came out again.

They remained only for a few moments on deck, and then resumed their game under the impression that the ship had stopped for reasons best known to the captain and not involving any danger to her. Later, in describing the scene that took place, M. Marechal, who was among the survivors, said: "When three-quarters of a mile away we stopped, the spectacle before our eyes was in its way magnificent. In a very calm sea, beneath a sky moonless but sown with millions of stars, the enormous Titanic lay on the water, illuminated from the water line to the boat deck. The bow was slowly sinking into the black water."

The tendency of the whole ship's company except the men in the engine department, who were made aware of the danger by the inrushing water, was to make light of it and in some instances even to ridicule the thought of danger to so substantial a fabric.

THE CAPTAIN ON DECK

When Captain Smith came from the chart room onto the bridge, his first words were, "Close the emergency doors."

"They're already closed, sir," Mr. Murdock replied.

"Send to the carpenter and tell him to sound the ship," was the next order. The message was sent to the carpenter, but the carpenter never came up to report. He was probably the first man on the ship to lose his life. The captain then looked at the communicator, which shows in what direction the ship is listing. He saw that she carried five degrees list to starboard.

The ship was then rapidly settling forward. All the steam sirens were blowing. By the captain's orders, given in the next few minutes, the engines were put to work at pumping out the ship, distress signals were sent by the Marconi, and rockets were sent up from the bridge by Quartermaster Rowe. All hands were ordered on deck.

PASSENGERS NOT ALARMED

The blasting shriek of the sirens had not alarmed the great company of the *Titanic*, because such steam calls are an incident of travel in seas where fogs roll. Many had gone to bed, but the hour, 11:40 P. M., was not too late for the friendly contact of saloons and smoking rooms. It was Sunday night and the ship's concert had ended, but there were many hundreds up and moving among the gay lights and many on deck with their eyes strained toward the mysterious west, where home lay. And in one jarring, breath-sweeping moment all of these, asleep or awake, were at the mercy of chance.

Few among the more than 2000 aboard could have had a thought of danger. The man, who had stood up in the smoking room to say that the *Titanic* was vulnerable or that in a few minutes two-thirds of her people would be face to face with death, would have been considered a fool or a lunatic. No ship ever sailed the seas that gave her passengers more confidence, more cool security.

Within a few minutes stewards and other members of the crew were sent round to arouse the people. Some utterly refused to get up. The stewards had almost to force the doors of the staterooms to make the somnolent appreciate their peril, and many of them, it is believed, were drowned like rats in a trap.

ASTOR AND WIFE STROLLED ON DECK

Colonel and Mrs. Astor were in their room and saw the ice vision flash by. They had not appreciably felt the gentle shock and supposed that nothing out of the ordinary had happened. They were both dressed and came on deck leisurely. William T. Stead, the London journalist, wandered on deck for a few minutes, stopping to talk to Frank Millet. "What do they say is the trouble?" he asked. "Icebergs," was the brief reply. "Well," said Stead, "I guess it is nothing serious. I'm going back to my cabin to read."

From end to end on the mighty boat officers were rushing about without much noise or confusion, but giving orders sharply. Captain Smith told the third officer to rush downstairs and see whether the water was coming in very fast. "And," he added, "take some armed guards along to see that the stokers and engineers stay at their posts."

In two minutes the officer returned. "It looks pretty bad, sir," he said. "The water is rushing in and filling the bottom. The locks of the water-tight compartments have been sprung by the shock."

"Give the command for all passengers to be on deck with life-belts on."

Through the length and breadth of the boat, upstairs and downstairs, on all decks, the cry rang out: "All passengers on deck with life-preservers."

A SUDDEN TREMOR OF FEAR

For the first time, there was a feeling of panic. Husbands sought for wives and children. Families gathered together. Many who were asleep hastily caught up their clothing and rushed on deck. A moment before the men had been joking about the life-belts, according to the story told by Mrs. Vera Dick, of Calgary, Canada. "Try this one," one man said to her, "they are the very latest thing this season. Everybody's wearing them now."

Another man suggested to a woman friend, who had a fox terrier in her arms, that she should put a life-saver on the dog. "It won't fit," the woman replied, laughing. "Make him carry it in his mouth," said the friend.

CONFUSION AMONG THE IMMIGRANTS

Below, on the steerage deck, there was intense confusion. About the time the officers on the first deck gave the order that all men should stand to one side and all women should go below to deck B, taking the children with them, a similar order was given to the steerage passengers. The women were ordered to the front, the men to the rear. Half a dozen healthy, husky immigrants pushed their way forward and tried to crowd into the first boat.

"Stand back," shouted the officers who were manning the boat. "The women come first."

Shouting curses in various foreign languages, the immigrant men continued their pushing and tugging to climb into the boats. Shots rang out. One big fellow fell over the railing into the water. Another dropped to the deck, moaning. His jaw had been shot away. This was the story told by the bystanders afterwards on the pier. One husky Italian told the writer on the pier that the way in which the men were shot down was horrible. His sympathy was with the men who were shot.

"They were only trying to save their lives," he said.

WIRELESS OPERATOR DIED AT HIS POST

On board the *Titanic*, the wireless operator, with a life-belt about his waist, was hitting the instrument that was sending out CQD.,(Come Quickly, Danger) messages, "Struck on iceberg, CQD"

"Shall I tell captain to turn back and help?" flashed a reply from the Carpathia.

"Yes, old man," the Titanic wireless operator responded. "Guess we're sinking."

On the deck where the first class passengers were quartered, known as deck A, there was none of the confusion that was taking place on the lower decks. The *Titanic* was standing without much rocking. The captain had given an order and the band was playing.

The RMS Olympic, the first of the Titanic class ships built by Harland & Wolff for the White Star Line.
Bain News Service photo courtesy of the Library of Congress.

A newspaper graphic of women of wealth and position who were on the Titanic.

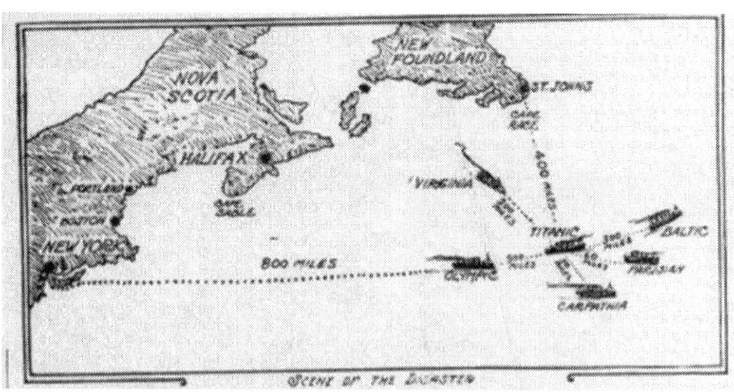

The point at which the Titanic hit the iceberg and other ships when the call for help went out.

"BE BRITISH": The Last Words of the "Titanic's" Captain.

"They that go down to the sea in ships, that do business in great waters."—Psalm cvii.

COMMANDER EDWARD J. SMITH, R.N.R.

From a portrait taken in New York. Reproduced by kind permission of Mrs. Smith

Born in the Year 1853

Nothing is here for tears, nothing to wail
Or knock the breast, no weakness, no contempt,
Dispraise or blame; nothing but well and fair,
And what may quiet us in a death so noble.—Samson Agonistes

Died April 15, 1912

Chapter IV
IN THE DRIFTING LIFE-BOATS

SIXTEEN boats were in the procession which entered on the terrible hours of rowing, drifting and suspense. Women wept for lost husbands and sons, sailors sobbed for the ship which had been their pride. Men choked back tears and sought to comfort the widowed. Perhaps, they said, other boats might have put off in another direction. They strove, though none too sure themselves, to convince the women of the certainty that a rescue ship would appear.

In the distance the *Titanic* looked an enormous length, her great bulk outlined in black against the starry sky, every porthole and saloon blazing with light. It was impossible to think anything could be wrong with such a leviathan, were it not for that ominous tilt downwards in the bows, where the water was now up to the lowest row of port-holes. Presently, about 2 A. M., as near as can be determined, those in the life-boats observed her settling very rapidly with the bows and the bridge completely under water, and concluded it was now only a question of minutes before she went.

So it proved she slowly tilted straight on end with the stern vertically upwards, and as she did, the lights in the cabins and saloons, which until then had not flickered for a moment, died out, came on again for a single flash, and finally went altogether. At the same time the machinery roared down through the vessel with a rattle and a groaning that could be heard for miles, the weirdest sound surely that could be heard in the middle of the ocean, a thousand miles away from land. But this was not yet quite the end.

Titanic Stood Upright

To the amazement of the awed watchers in the lifeboats, the doomed vessel remained in that upright position for a time estimated at five minutes; some in the boat say less, but it was certainly some minutes that at least 150 feet of the Titanic towered up above the level of the sea and loomed black against the sky.

SAW LAST OF BIG SHIP

Then with a quiet, slanting dive she disappeared beneath the waters, and the eyes of the helpless spectators had looked for the last time upon the gigantic vessel on which they had set out from Southampton. And there was left to the survivors only the gently heaving sea, the life-boats filled with men and women in every conceivable condition of dress and undress, above the perfect sky of brilliant stars with not a cloud, all tempered with a bitter cold that made each man and woman long to be one of the crew who toiled away with the oars and kept themselves warm thereby—a curious, deadening; bitter cold unlike anything they had felt before.

"ONE LONG MOAN"

And then with all these there fell on the ear the most appalling noise that human being has ever listened to—the cries of hundreds of fellow-beings struggling in the icy cold water, crying for help with a cry that could not be answered. Third Officer Herbert John Pitman, in charge of one of the boats, described this cry of agony in his testimony before the Senatorial Investigating Committee, under the questioning of Senator Smith:

"I heard no cries of distress until after the ship went down," he said.

"How far away were the cries from your life-boat?"

"Several hundred yards, probably, some of them."

"Describe the screams."

"Don't, sir, please! I'd rather not talk about it."

"I'm sorry to press it, but what was it like? Were the screams spasmodic?"

"It was one long continuous moan."

The witness said the moans and cries continued an hour. Those in the life-boats longed to return and pick up some of the poor drowning souls, but they feared this would mean swamping the boats and a further loss of life.

Some of the men tried to sing to keep the women from hearing the cries, and rowed hard to get away from the scene of the wreck, but the memory of those sounds will be one of the things the rescued will find it difficult to forget.

The waiting sufferers kept a lookout for lights, and several times it was shouted that steamers' lights were seen, but they turned out to be either a light from another boat or a star low down on the horizon. It was hard to keep up hope.

WOMEN TRIED TO COMMIT SUICIDE

"Let me go back—I want to go back to my husband—I'll jump from the boat if you don't," cried an agonized voice in one life-boat.

"You can do no good by going back—other lives will be lost if you try to do it. Try to calm yourself for the sake of the living. It may be that your husband will be picked up somewhere by one of the fishing boats."

The woman who pleaded to go back, according to Mrs. Vera Dick, of Calgary, Canada, later tried to throw herself from the life-boat. Mrs. Dick, describing the scenes in the life-boats, said there were half a dozen women in that one boat who tried to commit suicide when they realized that the *Titanic* had gone down.

"Even in Canada, where we have such clear nights," said Mrs. Dick, "I have never seen such a clear sky. The stars were very bright and we could see the Titanic plainly, like a great hotel on the water. Floor after floor of the lights went out as we watched. It was horrible, horrible. I can't bear to think about it. From the distance, as we rowed away, we could hear the band playing 'Nearer, My God to Thee.'

"Among the life-boats themselves, however, there were scenes just as terrible, perhaps, but to me nothing could outdo the tragic grandeur with which the Titanic went to its death. To realize it, you would have to see the Titanic as I saw it the day we set sail—with the flags flying and the bands playing. Everybody on board was laughing and talking about the Titanic being the biggest and most luxurious boat on the ocean and being unsinkable. To think of it then and to think of it standing out there in the night, wounded to death and gasping for life, is almost too big for the imagination.

SCANTILY CLAD WOMEN IN LIFE-BOATS

"The women on our boat were in nightgowns and bare feet—some of them—and the wealthiest women mingled with the poorest immigrants. One immigrant woman kept shouting: 'My God, my poor father! He put me in this boat and would not save himself. Oh, why didn't I die, why didn't I die? Why can't I die now?'

"We had to restrain her; else she would have jumped overboard. It was simply awful. Some of the men apparently had said they could row just to get into the boats. We paid no attention to cowardice, however. We were all busy with our own troubles. My heart simply bled for the women who were separated from their husbands.

"The night was frightfully cold, although clear. We had to huddle together to keep warm. Everybody drank sparingly of the water and ate sparingly of the bread. We did not know when we would be saved. Everybody tried to remain cool, except the poor creatures who could think of nothing but their own great loss. Those with the most brains seemed to control themselves best."

PHILADELPHIA WOMEN HEROINES

How Mrs. George D. Widener, whose husband and son perished after kissing her good-bye and helping her into one of the boats, rowed when exhausted seamen were on the verge of collapse, was told by Emily Geiger, maid of Mrs. Widener, who was saved with her. The girl said

Mrs. Widener bravely toiled throughout the night and consoled other women who had broken down under the strain.

Mrs. William E. Carter and Mrs. John B. Thayer were in the same life-boat and worked heroically to keep it free from the icy menace. Although Mrs. Thayer's husband remained aboard the *Titanic* and sank with it, and although she had no knowledge of the safety of her son until they met, hours later, aboard the *Carpathia*, Mrs. Thayer bravely labored at the oars throughout the night.

In telling of her experience Mrs. Carter said: "When I went over the side with my children and got in the boat there were no seamen in it. Then came a few men, but there were oars with no one to use them. The boat had been filled with passengers, and there was nothing else for me to do but to take an oar.

"We could see now that the time of the ship had come. She was sinking, and we were warned by cries from the men above to pull away from the ship quickly. Mrs. Thayer, wife of the vice-president of the Pennsylvania Railroad, was in my boat, and she, too, took an oar.

"It was cold and we had no time to clothe ourselves with warm overcoats. The rowing warmed me. We started to pull away from the ship. We could see the dim outlines of the decks above, but we could not recognize anybody."

MANY WOMEN ROWING

Mrs. William R. Bucknell's account of the part women played in the rowing is as follows:

"There were thirty-five persons in the boat in which the captain placed me. Three of these were ordinary seamen, supposed to manage the boat, and a steward.

"One of these men seemed to think that we should not start away from the sinking ship until it could be learned whether the other boats would accommodate the rest of the women. He seemed to think that; more could be crowded into ours, if necessary.

"'I would rather go back and go down with the ship than leave under these circumstances.' he cried.

"The captain shouted to him to obey orders and to pull for a little light that could just be discerned miles in the distance. I do not know what this little light was. It may have been a passing fishing vessel, which, of course could not know our predicament. Anyway, we never reached it.

"We rowed all night; I took an oar and sat beside the Countess de Rothes. Her maid had an oar and so did mine. The air was freezing cold, and it was not long before the only man that appeared to know anything about rowing commenced to complain that his hands were freezing: A woman back of him handed him a shawl from about her shoulders.

"As we rowed we looked back at the lights of the Titanic. There was not a sound from her, only the lights began to get lower and lower, and finally she sank. Then we heard a muffled explosion and a dull roar caused by the great suction of water.

"There was not a drop of water on our boat. The last minute before our boat was launched Captain Smith threw aboard a bag of bread. I took the precaution of taking a good drink of water before we started, so I suffered no inconvenience from thirst."

Mrs. Lucien Smith, whose young husband perished, was another heroine. It is related by survivors that she took turns at the oars, and then, when the boat was in danger of sinking, stood ready to plug a hole with her finger if the cork stopper became loose.

In another boat Mrs. Cornell and her sister, who had a slight knowledge of rowing, took turns at the oars, as did other women. The boat in which Mrs. J. J. Brown, of Denver, Col., was saved contained only three men in all, and only one rowed. He was a half-frozen seaman who was tumbled into the boat at the last minute. The woman wrapped him in blankets and set him at an oar to start his blood. The second man was too old to be of any use. The third was a coward.

Strange to say, there was room in this boat for ten other people. Ten brave men would have received the warmest welcome of their lives if they had been there. The coward, being a quartermaster and the assigned head of the boat, sat in the stern and steered. He was terrified, and the women had to fight against his pessimism while they tugged at the oars.

The women sat two at each oar. One held the oar in place, the other did the pulling. Mrs. Brown coached them and cheered them on. She told them that the exercise would keep the chill out of their veins, and she spoke hopefully of the likelihood that some vessel would answer the wireless calls. Over the frightful danger of the situation the spirit of this woman soared.

THE PESSIMIST

And the coward sat in his stern seat, terrified, his tongue loosened with fright. He assured them there was no chance in the world. He had had fourteen years' experience, and he knew. First, they would have to row one and a half miles at least to get out of the sphere of the suction, if they did not want to go down. They would be lost, and nobody would ever find them.

"Oh, we shall be picked up sooner or later," said some of the braver ones. No, said the man, there was no bread in the boat, no water; they would starve—all that big boatload wandering the high seas with nothing to eat, perhaps for days.

"Don't," cried Mrs. Brown. "Keep that to yourself, if you feel that way. For the sake of these women and children, be a man. We have a smooth sea and a fighting chance. Be a man."

But the coward only knew that there was no compass and no chart aboard. They sighted what they thought was a fishing smack on the horizon, showing dimly in the early dawn. The man at the rudder steered toward it, and the women bent to their oars again. They covered several miles in this way—but the smack faded into the distance. They could not see it any longer. And the coward said that everything was over.

They rowed back nine weary miles. Then the coward thought they must stop rowing, and lie in the trough of the waves until the *Carpathia* should appear. The women tried it for a few moments, and felt the cold creeping into their bodies. Though exhausted from the hard physical labor they thought work was better than freezing.

"Row again!" commanded Mrs. Brown.

"No, no, don't," said the coward."

"We shall freeze," cried several of the women together. "We must row. We have rowed all this time. We must keep on or freeze."

When the coward still demurred, they told him plainly and once for all that if he persisted in wanting them to stop rowing, they were going to throw him overboard and be done with him for good. Something about the look in the eye of that Mississippi-bred oarswoman, who seemed such a force among her fellows, told him that he had better capitulate. And he did.

COUNTESS ROTHES AN EXPERT OARSWOMAN

Miss Alice Farnam Leader, a New York physician, escaped from the *Titanic* on the same boat which carried the Countess Rothes. "The countess is an expert oarswoman," said Doctor Leader, "and thoroughly at home on the water. She practically took command of our boat when it was found that the seaman who had been placed at the oars could not row skillfully. Several of the women took their place with the countess at the oars and rowed in turns, while the weak and unskilled stewards sat quietly in one end of the boat."

HELP IN SIGHT

The survivors were in the life-boats until about 5.30 A. M. About 3 A. M. faint lights appeared in the sky and all rejoiced to see what was supposed to be the coming dawn, but after watching for half an hour and seeing no change in the intensity of the light, the disappointed sufferers realized it was the Northern Lights. Presently low down on the horizon they saw a light which slowly resolved itself into a double light, and they watched eagerly to see if the two lights would separate and so prove to be only two of the boats, or whether these lights would remain together, in which case they should expect them to be the lights of a rescuing steamer.

To the inexpressible joy of all, they moved as one! Immediately the boats were swung around and headed for the lights. Someone shouted: "Now, boys, sing!" and everyone not too weak broke into song with "Row for the shore, boys." Tears came to the eyes of all as they realized that safety was at hand. The song was sung, but it was a very poor imitation of the real thing, for quavering voices make poor songs. A cheer was given next, and that was better—you can keep in tune for a cheer.

THE "LUCKY THIRTEEN"

"Our rescuer showed up rapidly, and as she swung round we saw her cabins all alight, and knew she must be a large steamer. She was now motionless and we had to row to her. Just then day broke, a beautiful quiet dawn with faint pink clouds just above the horizon, and a new moon whose crescent just touched the horizon. 'Turn your money over, boys,' said our cheery steersman, 'that is, if you have any with you,' he added.

"We laughed at him for his superstition at such a time, but he countered very neatly by adding: 'Well, I shall never say again that 13 is an unlucky number; boat 13 has been the best friend we ever had.' Certainly the 13 superstition is killed forever in the minds of those who escaped from the *Titanic* in boat 13.

"As we neared the *Carpathia* we saw in the dawning light what we thought was a full-rigged schooner standing up near her, and presently behind her another, all sails set, and we said: 'They are fisher boats from the Newfoundland bank and have seen the steamer lying to and are standing by to help.' But in another five minutes the light shone pink on them and we saw they were icebergs towering many feet in the air, huge, glistening masses, deadly white, still, and peaked in a way that had easily suggested a schooner. We glanced round the horizon and there were others wherever the eye could reach. The steamer we had to reach was surrounded by them and we had to make a detour to reach her, for between her and us lay another huge berg."

A WONDERFUL DAWN

Speaking of the moment when the *Carpathia* was sighted. Mrs. J. J. Brown, who had cowed the driveling quartermaster, said: "Then, knowing that we were safe at last, I looked about me. The most wonderful dawn I have ever seen came upon us. I have just returned from Egypt. I have been all over the world, but I have never seen anything like this.

First the gray and then the flood of light. Then the sun came up in a ball of red fire. For the first time we saw where we were. Near us was open water, but on every side was ice. Ice ten feet high was everywhere, and to the right and left and back and front were icebergs. Some of them were mountain high. This sea of ice was forty miles wide, they told me. We did not wait for the *Carpathia* to come to us, we rowed to it.

We were lifted up in a sort of nice little sling that was lowered to us. After that it was all over. The passengers of the *Carpathia* were so afraid that we would not have room enough that they gave us practically the whole ship to ourselves." It had been learned that some of the passengers, in fact all of the women passengers of the *Titanic* who were rescued, refer to "Lady Margaret," as they called Mrs. Brown as the strength of them all.

TRANSFERRING THE RESCUED

Officers of the *Carpathia* report that when they reached the scene of the Titanic's wreck there were fifty bodies or more floating in the sea. Only one mishap attended the transfer of the rescued from the lifeboats. One large collapsible life-boat, in which thirteen persons were seated, turned turtle just as they were about to save it, and all in it were lost.

THRILLING ACCOUNT OF RESCUE

Mr. Wallace Bradford, of San Francisco, a passenger aboard the *Carpathia*, gave the following thrilling account of the rescue of the Titanic's passengers.

"Since half-past four this morning I have experienced one of those never-to-be-forgotten circumstances that weighs heavy on my soul and which shows most awfully what poor things we mortals are. Long before this reaches you the news will be flashed that the Titanic has gone down and that our steamer, the *Carpathia*, caught the wireless message when seventy-five miles away and so far we have picked up twenty boats estimated to contain about 750 people.

"None of us can tell just how many, as they have been hustled to various staterooms and to the dining saloons to be warmed up. I was awakened by unusual noises and imagined that I smelled smoke. I jumped up and looked out of my port-hole, and saw a huge iceberg looming up like a rock off shore. It was not white, and I was positive that it was a rock, and the thought flashed through my mind, how in the world can we be near a rock when we are four days out from New York in a southerly direction and in mid-ocean.

"When I got out on deck the first man I encountered told me that the Titanic had gone down and we were rescuing the passengers.

“The first two boats from the doomed vessel were in sight making toward us. Neither of them was crowded. This was accounted for later by the fact that it was impossible to get many to leave the steamer, as they would not believe that she was going down. It was a glorious, clear morning and a quiet sea. Off to the starboard was a white area of ice plain, from whose even surface rose mammoth forts, castles and pyramids of solid ice almost as real as though they had been placed there by the hand of man.

"Our steamer was hove to about two and a half miles from the edge of this huge iceberg. The Titanic struck about 11.20 P. M. and did not go down until two o'clock. Many of the passengers were in evening dress when they came aboard our ship, and most of these were in a most bedraggled condition. Near me as I write is a girl about eighteen years old in a fancy dress costume of bright colors, while in another seat nearby is a women in a white dress trimmed with lace and covered with jaunty blue flowers.

"As the boats came alongside after the first two all of them contained a very large proportion of women. In fact, one of the boats had women at the oars, one in particular containing, as near as I could estimate, about forty-five women and only about six men. In this boat two women were handling one of the oars. All of the engineers went down with the steamer.

“Four bodies have been brought aboard. One is that of a fireman, who is said to have been shot by one of the officers because he refused to obey orders. Soon after I got on deck I could, with the aid of my glasses, count seven boats headed our way, and they continued to come up to half past eight o'clock. Some were in sight for a long time and moved very slowly, showing plainly that the oars were being handled by amateurs or by women.

"No baggage of any kind was brought by the survivors. In fact, the only piece of baggage that reached the Carpathia from the Titanic is a small closed trunk about twenty-four inches square, evidently the property of an Irish female immigrant. While some seemed fully dressed, many of the men having their overcoats and the women sealskin and other coats, others came just as they had jumped from their berths, clothed in their pajamas and bath robes."

THE SORROW OF THE LIVING

Of the survivors in general it may be said that they escaped death and they gained life. Life is probably sweet to them as it is to everyone, but what physical and mental torture has been the price of life to those who were brought back to land on the Carpathia—the hours in life-boats, amid the crashing of ice, the days of anguish that have succeeded, the horrors of body and mind still experienced and never to be entirely absent until death affords them its relief.

The thought of the nation to-day is for the living. They need our sympathy, our consolation more than do the dead, and, perhaps, in the majority of the cases they need our protecting care as well.

1912 U.S. Senate Recommendations—

1. It is recommended that all ships carrying more than 100 passengers shall have two searchlights.
2. That a revision be made of steamship inspection laws of foreign countries to conform to the standard proposed in the United States.
3. That every ship be required to carry sufficient lifeboats for all passengers and crew.
4. That the use of wireless be regulated to prevent interference by amateurs, and that all ships have a wireless operator on constant duty.
5. Detailed recommendations are made as to water-tight bulkhead construction on ocean-going ships. Bulkheads should be so spaced that any two adjacent compartments of a ship might be flooded without sinking.
6. Transverse bulkheads forward and abaft the machinery should be continued watertight to the uppermost continuous structural deck, and this deck should be fitted water-tight.

A crowd of thousands awaited the arrival of the Carpathia at the Cunard line terminal in New York.

2 THE SPHERE [Supplement to The Sphere, April 27, 1912

THE MECHANISM BY WHICH THE BOATS WERE LOWERED.

A PAIR OF THE WELIN DAVITS ON BOARD THE "TITANIC"

R. Welch, Belfast

The Welin davit, which was fitted to the "Titanic" and is also found on a large number of the latest type of passenger liners, is the ingenious invention of Mr. Axel Welin. The davit is carried over the side by turning the gun-metal screw, seen in the centre of the picture. The bottom of the quadrant is a cog which, working on a base point, forms a double action, thus throwing the davit outwards to its extreme limit is a matter of moments. The old-type davit has to be completely turned in two operations which take a considerable amount of time

The Cunard liner Carpathia as it docked in New York with the 705 survivors of the Titanic on board.

The crew of a boat from the rescue ship Minia fishes a Titanic passenger's body out of the ocean.
Photo courtesy of National Maritime Museum, Halifax, NS.

Coffins unloaded from the cable ship MacKay-Bennett in Halifax. 328 bodies were recovered, the MacKay-Bennett only had enough supplies to process 153 bodies for burial, and the others were buried at sea.

The Carpathia approaches port with the Titanic lifeboats hanging from its decks.

The Times Dispatch

Carpathia Refuses to Give Any Details of Titanic's Loss and as Fruitless Hours Go By, Suspense Grows More Maddening

NO NEWS COMES ON WHICH HOPE MAY BE RAISED

CROWD OF MORBID EXPECTED AT PIER

NO FALLING OFF IN OCEAN TRAVEL

GREAT SHIP RENT ALMOST ASUNDER

FAMILIES OF CREW IN GREAT DESPAIR

ISMAY MUST TELL HOW HE ESCAPED

Frustration over the lack of news from the Carpathia angered many including President Taft.

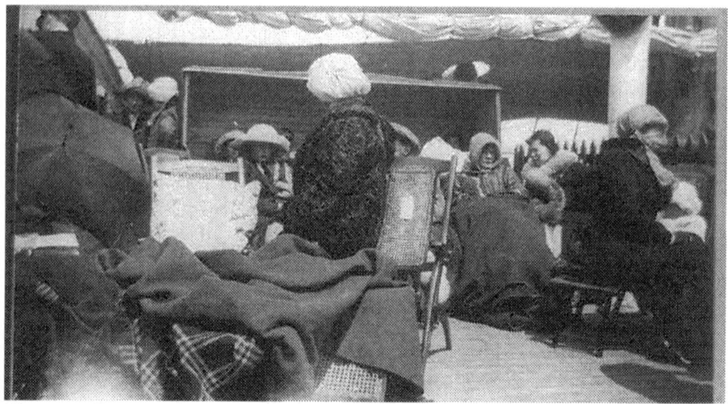

Group of rescued survivors on the Carpathia.

Two young French boys were taken by their father on board the Titanic. When the ship began to sink, the man handed them down to a lifeboat and they were saved

HMHS Britannic was the third in the series of Titanic class ships. The Britannic was appropriated by the British government for use as a hospital ship.

Capt. Arthur Henry Rostron and the officers of the Carpathia accept this loving cup from the grateful survivors of the Titanic.

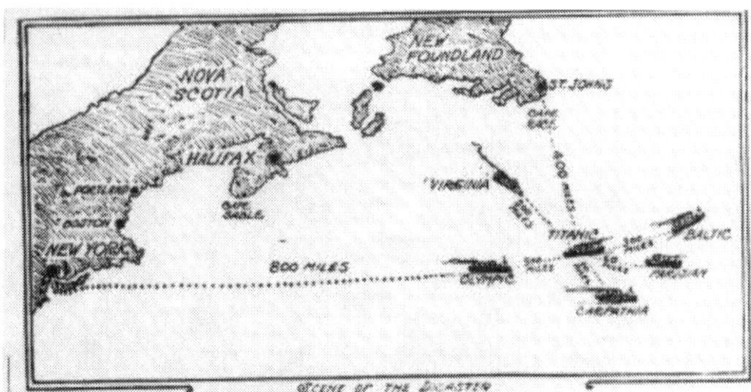

This map from 1912 shows the position of the Titanic when it hit the ice berg as well as nearby ships.

San Francisco Examiner — April 19, 1912.

Frederick Fleet, a lookout on the Titanic. He testified that he had given three warnings of ice ahead to the bridge which were ignored.

Unsettled Today
Fair Tomorrow

Virginian-Pilot.

THE NORFOLK LANDMARK

NORFOLK, VA., TUESDAY, APRIL 16, 1912. FOURTEEN PAGES.

VOL. XLIII. NO. 16.

OVER FIFTEEN HUNDRED SANK TO DEATH WITH GIANT WHITE STAR STEAMER TITANIC

Horrible Disaster Greatest In Marine History of World

Floating Hotel In Collision With Iceberg Early Yesterday Morning Off New Foundland Banks

VESSEL REMAINED AFLOAT FOUR HOURS AFTER CRASH

Men of World-Wide Prominence Among First Class Passengers--Gay New York Stunned By Awfulness of Disaster

THE WRECK OF THE
TITANIC
A DESCRIPTIVE PIANO COMPOSITION
BY
JEANETTE FORREST
McKinley Music Co.
CHICAGO — NEW YORK

Titanic survivors in lifeboat as they came alongside the Carpathia.

Survivors row to the side of the Carpathia.

A crowd gathers and is awaiting the news from the Carpathia at the White Star office in New York.

The mother of the two French boys who lived after their father perished on the Titanic. Their mother saw the photo which was widely circulated in Europe and she went to New York to retrieve them.

La America — La America

לה אמיריקה

טיריבלי קאטאסטרופה אין איל אטלאנטיק

איל מאס גראנדי באפור דיל מונדו "טיטאניק" סי אונדיו

Newspapers in every language reported on the Titanic disaster. This one was in Hebrew.

Mrs. John Jacob Astor, 19, survived the disaster. Her husband gallantly supervised the loading of lifeboats and stood aside to die on the Titanic. He was a wealthy real estate tycoon and former congressman.

Funeral of Col. Astor took place on May 4, 1912 after his body was discovered.

Maj. Archibald Butt, right, was the chief of staff to President William Howard Taft, left. Butt helped to load the lifeboats with women and told a music teacher he knew from the White House to "please give my best to the folks back home".

Mrs. J. J. (Margaret) Brown, of Denver, Colorado. She was known forever as the 'Unsinkable Molly Brown'. She took charge of a lifeboat which had but three men in it and ordered the women to take turns rowing and save themselves from freezing to death.

Father Frank Browne took photos of the Titanic at sea, the only ones to survive the disaster. Father Browne was given a trip from Southampton to Ireland by his uncle and also had a camera. The entire collection of photos is now on display in Ireland. These passengers were from steerage and were enjoying the sun. Father Browne served in the British Army as a chaplain during WWI and was highly decorated. His photos of the Titanic were printed around the world and he gave lectures on the ship sinking for years.

The young lad shown in this photo survived along with his father, to his left. The boy died when hit by a car four years later and his father drowned in a swimming pool one year afterwards. The collection is available for view at the Cobh Ireland Heritage Center as well as on display the Titanic Museums in Pigeon Forge, TN and Branson, MO.

Two lifeboats approach the Carpathia. The one on right shows that those on board were able to assemble the sail. There were no lanterns on the lifeboats and the crew had no training on how to deploy them.

A Titanic victim is embalmed on the MacKay-Bennett was it is still at sea.

CARPATHIA DODGED 20 BERGS IN WILD DASH TO AID TITANIC

FINAL EDITION

The World.

EXTRA

NEW YORK, FRIDAY, APRIL 19, 1912.

TITANIC'S 1,476 DEAD AWFUL SACRIFICE TO OCEAN SPEED MANIA

Hurled Against Iceberg at 23 Knots an Hour to Establish Reputation for New and Biggest Liner.

FIRST OFFICER OF TITANIC SHOT HIMSELF ON BRIDGE

THRILLING STORY OF RESCUE TOLD BY CARPATHIA'S SKIPPER

Little French Children Thrown By Father From Liner to Safety

Capt. Rostron Describes Before Senate Investigators Daring Dash in Spite of Peril in Response to Titanic's Call for Help.

ISMAY MAKES DENIAL OF ALL RESPONSIBILITY

Mr. Rayner Bitterly Arraigns Managing Director in a Speech Before the Senate in Washington.

FATHER TOSSED HIS BABIES FROM TITANIC TO LIFEBOAT

French and British soldiers read news of the war.

Chapter V
Two Years After Titanic; War Begins!

When the people of the United States heard the news of the assassination of Archduke Francis Ferdinand, heir to the throne of Austria-Hungary, and his wife in Sarajevo, Bosnia, on June 28, 1914, it was with a feeling of great regret that another sorrow had been added to the many already born by the aged Emperor Francis Joseph. That those fatal shots would echo around the world and, flashing out suddenly like a bolt from the blue, hurl nearly the whole of Europe within a week's time from a state of profound peace into one of continental war, unannounced, unexpected, unexplained, unprecedented in suddenness and enormity, was an unimaginable possibility.

And yet the ringing of the church bells was suddenly drowned by the roar of cannon, the voice of the dove of peace by the blare of the trump of war, and throughout the world ran a shudder of terror at these unwonted and ominous sounds.

But in looking back through history, tracing the course of events during the past century, following the footsteps of men in war and peace from that day of upheaval when medieval feudalism went down in disarray before the arms of the people in the French Revolution, some explanation of the Great European war of 1914 may be reached. Every event in history has its roots somewhere in earlier history, and we need but dig deep enough to find them.

The French Revolution stood midway between two spheres of history, the sphere of medieval barbarism and that of modern enlightenment. It exploded like a bomb in the midst of the self-satisfied aristocracy of the earlier social system and rent it into the fragments which no hand could put together again.

In this sense the career of Napoleon seems providential. The era of popular government had replaced that of autocratic and aristocratic government in France, and the armies of Napoleon spread these radical ideas throughout Europe until the oppressed people of every nation began to look upward with hope and see in the distance before them a haven of justice in the coming realm of human rights.

It required considerable time for these new conceptions to become thoroughly disseminated. A down-trodden people enchained by the theory of the "divine right of kings" to autocratic rule, had to break the fetters one by one and gradually emerge from a state of practical serfdom to one of enlightened emancipation. There were many setbacks, and progress was distressingly slow but nevertheless sure.

The story of this upward progress is the history of the nineteenth century, regarded from the special point of view of political progress and the development of human rights.

Gradually the autocrat has declined in power and authority, and the principle of popular rights has risen into view. This war will not have been fought in vain if, as predicted, it will result in the complete downfall of autocracy as a political principle, and the rise of the rule of the people, so that the civilized nations of the earth may never again be driven into a frightful war of extermination against peaceful neighbors at the nod of a hereditary sovereign.

Chapter VI
DRAMATIC SUDDENNESS OF THE OUTBREAK

On the night of July 25th 1914 the people of the civilized world settled down to restful slumbers, with no dreams of the turmoil that was ready to burst forth. On the morning of the 26th they rose to learn that a great war had begun, a conflict the possible width and depth of which no man was yet able to foresee; and as day after day passed on, each day some new nation springing into the terrible arena until practically the whole of Europe was in arms and the Armageddon seemed at hand, the world stood amazed and astounded, wondering what hand had loosed so vast a catastrophe, what deep and secret causes lay below the ostensible causes of the war.

The causes of this were largely

unknown. As a panic at times affects a vast assemblage, with no one aware of its origin, so a wave of hostile sentiment may sweep over vast communities until the air is full of urgent demands for war with scarce a man knowing why.

What is already said only feebly outlines the state of consternation into which the world was cast in that fateful week in which the doors of the Temple of Janus, long closed, were suddenly thrown wide open and the terrible God of War marched forth, the whole earth trembling beneath his feet. It was the breaking of a mighty storm in a placid sky, the fall of a meteor which spreads terror and destruction on all sides, the explosion of a vast bomb in a great assemblage; it was everything that can be imagined of the sudden and overwhelming, of the amazing and incredible.

TRADE AND COMMERCE PARALYZED

For the moment the world stood still, plunged into a panic that stopped all its activities. The stock exchanges throughout the nations were closed, to prevent that wild and hasty action which precipitates disaster. Throughout

Europe trade, industry, commerce all ceased, paralyzed at their sources. No ship of any of the nations concerned except Britain dared venture from port, lest it should fall a prey to the prowling sea dogs of war which made all the oceans unsafe. The hosts of American tourists who had gone abroad under the sunny skies of peace suddenly beheld the dark clouds of war rolling overhead, blotting out the sun, and casting their black shadows over all things fair.

What does this state of affairs, this sudden stoppage of the wheels of industry, this unforeseen and wide spread of the conditions of war portend? Emerson has said: "When a great thinker comes into the world all things are at risk." There is potency in this, and also in a variation of Emerson's text which we shall venture to make: "When a great war comes upon the world all things are at risk." Everything which we have looked upon as fixed and stable quakes as if from mighty hidden forces. The whole world stands irresolute and amazed. The steady-going habits and occupations of peace cease or are perilously threatened, and no one can be sure of escaping from some of the dire effects of the catastrophe.

WIDESPREAD INFLUENCES

The conditions of production vanish, to be replaced by conditions of destruction. That which had been growing in grace and beauty for years is overturned and destroyed in a moment of ravage. Changes of this kind are not confined to the countries in which the war rages or the cities which conquering column of troops occupy. They go beyond the borders of military activity; they extend to far-off quarters of the earth. We quote from *The New York World* a vivid picture drawn at the opening of the great

European war. Its motto is "all the world is paying the cost of the folly of Europe."

Never before was war made so swiftly wide. News of it comes from Japan, from Porto Rico, from Africa, from places where in old days news of hostilities might not travel for months.

"Non-combatants are in the vast majority, even in the countries at war, but they are not immune to its blight. Austria is isolated from the world because her ally, Germany, will take no chances of spilling military information and will not forward mails. If, telephoning in France, you use a single foreign word, even an English one, your wire is cut. Hans the German waiter, Franz the clarinetist in the little street band, is locked up as a possible spy.

There are great German business houses in London and Paris; their condition is that of English and French business houses in Berlin, and that is not pleasant. Great Britain contemplates, as an act of war, the voiding of patents held by Germans in the United Kingdom. Nothing is too petty, nothing too great, nothing too distant in kind or miles from the field of war to feel its influence. The whole world is the loser by it, whoever at the end of all the battles may say that he has won.

DILEMMA OF THE TOURISTS

Let us consider one of the early results of the war. It vitally affected great numbers of Americans, the army of tourists who had made their way abroad for rest, study and recreation and whose numbers, while unknown, were great, some estimating them at the high total of 100,000 or more.

These, scattered over all sections of Europe, some with money in abundance, some with just enough for a brief journey, capitalists, teachers, students, all were caught in the sudden flurry of the war, their letters of credit useless, transportation difficult or impossible to obtain, all exposed to inconveniences, some to indignities, some of them on the flimsiest pretense seized and searched as spies, the great mass of them thrown into a state of panic that added greatly to the unpleasantness of the situation in which they found themselves.

While these conditions of panic gradually adjusted themselves, the status of the tourists continued difficult and annoying. The railroads were seized for the transportation of troops, leaving many Americans helplessly held in far interior parts, frequently without money or credit. One example of the difficulties encountered will serve as an instance which might be repeated a hundred fold.

Seven hundred Americans from Geneva were made by Swiss troops to leave a train. Many who refused were forced off at the point or by guns. This compulsory removal took place at some distance from a station near the border, according to Mrs. Edward Collins, of New York, who with her three daughters was on the train. With 200 others they reached Paris and were taken aboard a

French troop train. Most of the arrivals were women; the men were left behind because of lack of space.

One hundred women refused to take the train without their husbands; scores struck back for Geneva; others on foot, carrying articles of baggage, started in the direction of Paris, hoping to get trains somewhere. Just why Swiss troops thus occupied themselves is not explained; but in times of warlike turmoil many unexplainable things occur.

Here is an incident of a different kind, told by one of the escaping host: "I went into the restaurant car for lunch," he said. "When I tried to return to the car where I'd left my suitcase, hat, cane and overcoat, I couldn't find it. Finally the conductor said blithely, 'Oh, that car was taken off for the use of the army.'

"I was forced to continue traveling coatless, hatless and minus my baggage until I boarded the steamer *FLUSHING*, when I managed to swipe a straw hat during the course of the Channel passage while the people were down eating in the saloon. I grabbed the first one on the hat rack. Talk about a romantic age. Why, I wouldn't live in any other time than now. We will be boring our grandchildren talking about this war."

The scarcity of provisions in many localities and the withholding of money by the banks made the situation, as regarded Americans, especially serious. Those fortunate enough to reach port without encountering these difficulties found the situation there equally

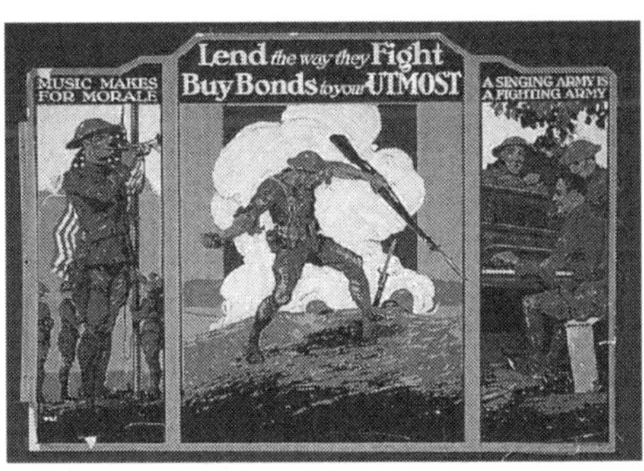

embarrassing. The great German and English liners, for instance, were held up by order of the government, or feared to sail lest they should be taken captive by hostile cruisers.

Many of these lay in port in New York, forbidden to sail for fear of capture. These included ships of the Cunard and International Marine lines, the north German Lloyd, the Hamburg-American, the Russian-American, and the French lines, until then this port led the world in the congestion of great liners rendered inactive by the war situation abroad.

The few ships that put to sea were utterly incapable of accommodating a tithe of the anxious and appealing applicants. It had ceased, in the state of panic that prevailed, to be a mere question of money. Frightened millionaires were credited with begging for steerage berths. Everywhere was dread and confusion, men and women being in a state of mind past the limits of calm reasoning. Impulse is the sole ruling force where reason has ceased to act.

Time passed! Slowly the skies cleared; calmer conditions began to prevail. The United States government sent the battleship *USS TENNESSEE* abroad with several millions of dollars for the aid of destitute travelers and the relief of those who could not get their letters or credit and travelers' checks cashed. Such a measure of relief was necessary, there being people abroad with letters of credit for as much as $5,000 without money enough to buy a meal.

One tourist said: "I had to give a Milwaukee doctor, who had a letter of credit for $2,500 enough money to get shaved." London hotels showed much consideration for the needs of travelers without ready cash, but on the continent there were many such who were refused hotel accommodation.

As for those who reached New York or other American ports, many had fled in such haste as to leave their baggage behind. Numbers of the poorer travelers had exhausted their scanty stores of cash in the effort to escape from Europe and reached port utterly penniless. This called for immediate and an adequate solution and the governmental and moneyed interests on this side did their utmost to cope with the situation.

Vessels of American register were too few to carry the host applying for transportation, and it was finally decided to charter foreign vessels for this purpose and thus hasten the work of moving the multitude of appealing tourists. From 15,000 to 20,000 of these needed immediate attention, a majority of them being destitute.

Troops of the Black Watch march for voyage to France in 1914 as war began.

Chapter VII

More Troubles for the Tourists

Men and women needed not only transportation, but money also, and in this there is an interesting story to tell. The German steamer *KRONPRINZESSIN CECILIE*, bound for Bremen, had sailed from New York before the outbreak of the war, carrying about 1,200 passengers and a precious freight of gold, valued at $10,700,000. The value of the vessel herself added $5,000,000 to this sum. What had become of her and her tempting cargo was for a time unknown.

There were rumors that she had been captured by a British cruiser, but this had no better foundation than such rumors usually have. Her captain was alert to the situation, being informed by wireless of the sudden change from peace to war. One such message, received from an Irish wireless station, conveyed an order from the Bremen Company for him to return with all haste to an American port.

It was on the evening of Friday, July 31st, that this order came. At once the vessel changed its course. One by one the ship's lights were put out. The decks which could not be made absolutely dark were enclosed with canvas. By midnight the ship was as dark as the sea surrounding her.

On she went through Saturday and on Sunday ran into a dense fog. Through this she rushed with unchecked speed and in utter silence, not a toot coming from her fog-horn. This was all very well as a measure of secrecy, but it opened the way to serious danger through a possible collision, and a committee of passengers was formed to request the captain to reconsider his action.

Just as the committee reached his room the first blast of the fog-horn was heard, its welcome tone bringing a sense of security where grave apprehension had prevailed. A group of financiers were on board who offered to buy the ship and sail her under American colors. But to all such proposals Captain Polack turned a deaf ear. He said that his duty was spelled by his orders from Bremen to turn back and save his ship, and these he proposed to obey.

A passenger stated: "There were seven of the crew on watch all the time, two aloft. This enabled the captain to know of passing vessels before they came above the horizon. We were undoubtedly in danger on Sunday afternoon. We intercepted a wireless message in French in which two French cruisers were exchanging data in regard to their positions.

"The captain told me that he imagined those to be two vessels that regularly patrolled the fishing grounds in the interest of French fisheries. If the captain of either of those vessels should have come out of the fog and found us, his share of the prize in money might have amounted to $4,000,000. Did privateer ever dream of such booty!

"Early on Saturday our four great funnels were given broad black bands in order to make us look like the *Olympic,* which was supposed to be twenty-four hours ahead of us. There was a certain grim humor in the fact that the wireless operator on the *Olympic* kept calling us all Friday night. Of course we did not answer."

On Tuesday, August 4th, the great ship came within sight of land at the little village of Bar Harbor, Mount Desert Island, off the coast of Maine; a port scarcely large enough to hold the giant liner that had sought safety in its waters. Wireless messages were at once flashed to all parts of the country and the news that the endangered vessel, with its precious cargo, was now safe was received with general relief.

As regards the future movements of the ship Captain Polack said: "I can see no possibility of taking this ship to New York from here with safety. To avoid foreign vessels we should have to keep within the three - mile limit and to accomplish this; the ship would have to be built like a canoe. We have reached an American port in safety and that was more than I dared to hope. We have been in almost constant danger of capture, and we can consider ourselves extremely lucky to have come out so well.

I know I have been criticized for making too great speed under bad weather conditions, but I have not willfully endangered the lives of the passengers. I would rather have lost the whole cargo than have assumed any such risk. Of course, aside from this consideration, my one aim has been to save my ship and my cargo from capture.

I have not been acting on my own initiative, but under orders from the North German Lloyd in Bremen, and although I am an officer in the German navy my duty has been to the steamship line."

CLOSING THE STOCK MARKETS

We have so far dealt with only a few of the results of the war. There were various others of great moment, to some of which a passing allusion has been made. On July 30th, for the first time in history, the stock markets of the world were all closed at the same time. Heretofore when the European markets have been closed those on this side of the ocean remained open.

The New York Exchange was the last big stock market to announce temporary suspension of business. The New York Cotton Exchange closed, following the announcement of the failure of several brokerage firms. Stock Exchanges throughout the United States followed the example set by New York. The Stock Exchanges in London and the big provincial cities, as well as those on the Continent, ceased business, owing to the breakdown of the credit system, which was made complete by the postponement of the Paris settlement.

Depositors stormed every bank in London for gold, and the runs continued for a couple of days. In order to protect its dwindling gold supply the Bank of England raised its discount rate to 8 percent. Leading bankers of London requested Premier Asquith to suspend the bank act, and he promised to lay the matter before the Chancellor of the Exchequer. In all the capitals of Europe financial transactions virtually came to a standstill.

The slump in the market value of securities within the first week of the war flurry was estimated at $2,000,000,000, and radical measures were necessary to prevent hasty action while the condition of panic prevailed.

This sudden stoppage of ordinary financial operations was accompanied by a similar cessation of the industries of peace over a wide range of territory. The artisan was forced to let fall the tools of his trade and take up those of war. The railroads were similarly denuded of their employees except in so far as they were needed to convey soldiers and military supplies.

The customary uses of the railroad were largely suspended and travel went on under great difficulties. In a measure it had returned to the conditions existing before the invention of the locomotive. Even horse traffic was limited by the demands of the army for these animals, and foot travel regained some of its old ascendency.

War makes business active in one direction and in one only, that of army and navy supply, of the manufacture of the implements of destruction, of vast quantities of explosives, of multitudes of death-dealing weapons. Food supplies need to be diverted in the same direction, the demands of the soldier being considered first; -- those of the home people last, the latter being often supplied at starvation prices. There is plenty of work to do – of its kind. But it is of a kind that injures instead of aiding the people of the nations.

TERRIBLE EFFECTS OF WAR

This individual source of misery and suffering in war times is accompanied by a more direct one, that of the main purpose of war - destruction of human life and of property that might be utilized by an enemy, frequently by merciless pillage and devastation. It is horrible to think of the frightful suffering caused by every great battle.

Immediate death on the field might reasonably be welcomed as an escape from the suffering arising from wounds, the terrible mutilations, the injuries that rankle throughout life, the conversion of able-bodied men into feeble invalids, to be kept by the direct aid of their fellows or the indirect aid of the people at large through a system of pensions.

The physical sufferings of the soldiers from wounds and privations are perhaps not the greatest. Side by side with them are the mental anxieties of their families at home, their terrible suspense, and the effect upon them of tidings of the maiming or death of those dear to them or on whose labor they immediately depend. The harvest of misery arising from this cause it is impossible to estimate.

It is not to be seen in the open. It dwells unseen in humble homes, in city, village, or field, borne often uncomplainingly, but not less poignant from this cause. The tears and terrors thus produced are beyond calculation. But while the glories of war are celebrated with blast of trumpet and roll of drum, the terrible accompaniment of groans of misery is too apt to pass unheard and die away forgotten.

To turn from this roll of horrors, there are costs of war in other directions to be considered. Those include the ravage of cities by flame or pillage, the loss of splendid works of architecture, the irretrievable destruction of great productions of art, the vanishing of much on which the world had long set store.

Chapter VIII Terrible Cost of War-

THE TIDE OF DESTRUCTION

Not only on land, but at sea as well, the tide of destruction rises and swells. Huge warships, built at a cost of millions of dollars and tenanted by hundreds of hardy sailors, are torn and rent by shot and shell and at times sent to the bottom with all on board by the explosion of torpedoes beneath their unprotected lower hulls.

The torpedo boat, the submarine, with other agencies of unseen destruction, have come into play to add enormously to the horrors of naval warfare, while the bomb-dropping airships, letting fall its dire missiles from the sky, has come to add to the dread terror and torment of the battle-field.

We began this chapter with a statement of the startling suddenness of this Great War, and the widespread consequences which immediately followed. We have been led into a discussion of its issues, of the disturbing and distracting consequences which cannot fail to follow any great modern war between civilized nations.

We had some examples of this on a small scale in the recent Balkan-Turkish war. But that was of minor importance and its effects, many of them sanguinary and horrible, were mainly confined to the region in which it occurred. But a war covering nearly a whole continent cannot be confined in its consequences. All the world must feel them -though diminishing with distance.

The vast expanse of water which separates the United States from the European continent could not save its citizens from feeling certain ill effects from the struggle of war lords. America and Europe are tied together with many cords of business and interest, and the severing or weakening of these cannot fail to be seriously felt. Canada, at a similar width of removal from Europe, had reason to feel it still more seriously, from its close political relations with Great Britain.

In these days in which we live the cost of war is a giant to be reckoned with. With every increase in the size of cannon, the tonnage of warships, the destructiveness of weapons and ammunition, this element of cost grows proportionately greater and has in our day become stupendous.

Nations may spend in our era more cold cash in a day of war than would have served for a year in the famous days of chivalry. A study of this question was made by army and navy experts in 1914, and they decided that the expense to the five nations concerned in the European war would be not less than $50,000,000 a day.

If we add to this the loss of untold numbers of young men in the prime of life, whose labor is needed in the fields and workshops of the nations involved, other billions of dollars must be added to the estimate, due to the crippling of industries. There is also the destruction of property to be considered, including the very costly modern battleships, this also footing up into the billions.

When it is considered that in thirteen years the cost of maintenance of the armies and navies of the warring countries, as well as the cost of naval construction, exceeded $20,000,000,000 some idea may be had of the expense attached to war and the preparations of European countries for just such contingencies as those that arose in Europe in 1914.

The cost of the Panama Canal, one of the most useful aids to the commerce of the world, was approximately $375,000,000, but the expense of the preparations for war in Europe during the time it took to build the canal exceeded the cost of this gigantic undertaking nearly sixty to one. The money thus expended on preparation for war during the thirteen years named would, if spent in railroad and marine construction, have given vast commercial power to these nations.

To what extent have they been benefited by the rivalry to gain precedence in military power? They stand on practically the same basis now that it is all at an end. Would they not be on the same basis if it had never begun? Aside from this is the incentive to employ these vast armaments in the purpose for which they were designed, the effect of creating a military spirit and developing a military caste in each by the nations, a result very likely to produce ill effects.

The total expense of maintenance of armies and navies, together with the cost of construction in thirteen years, in Germany, Austria, Russia, France and Great Britain, was as follows:

Naval expenditures	**$5,648,525,000**
Construction	**2,146,765,000**
Cost of armies	**13,138,403,000**
Total	**$20,933,693,000**

The wealth of the same nations in round figures is:

Great Britain	**$80,000,000,000**
Germany	**60,500,000,000**
Austria	**25,000,000,000**
France	**65,000,000,000**

Russia	**40,000,000,000**
Total	**270,500,000,000**

This enormous expense which was incurred in preparation for war needed to be rapidly increased to meet the expenses of actual warfare. The British House of Commons authorized war credits amounting to $1,025,000,000, while the German Reichstag voted $1,250,000,000. Austria and France had to set aside vast sums for their respective war chests.

HALF CENTURY TO PAY DEBTS

In anticipation of trouble Germany in 1913 voted $250,000,000 for extraordinary war expenses and about $100,000,000 was spent on an aerial fleet. France spent $60,000,000 for the same purpose.

The annual cost of maintaining the great armies and navies of Europe even on a peace basis is enormous, and it must be vastly increased during war. The official figures for 1913-14 are:

British army	**$224,300,000**
British navy	**224,140,000**
German army	**183,090,000**
German navy	**111,300,000**
French army	**191,431,580**
French navy	**119,571,400**
Russian army	**317,800,000**
Russian navy	**122,500,000**
Austrian army	**82,300,000**
Austrian navy	**42,000,000**
Total	**$1,618,432,980**

It was evident that taxes to meet the extraordinary expenses of war would have to be greatly increased in Germany and France. As business became at a standstill throughout Europe and every port of entry blocked, experts wondered where the money was to come from.

All agreed that, when peace should be declared and the figures were all in, the result financially would be staggering and that the heaviest burden it had ever borne would rest upon Europe for fifty years to come. For when the roar of the cannon ceases and the nations are at rest, then dawns the era of payment, inevitable, inescapable, one in which for generations every man and woman must share.

Chapter IX
Fundamental Causes of the Conflagration

What brought on the mighty war which so suddenly sprang forth? What evident, what subtle, what deep-hidden causes led to this sudden demolition of the temple of peace? What pride of power, what lust of ambition, what desire of imperial dominion cast the armed nations into the field of conflict, on which multitudes of innocent victims were to be sacrificed to satiate the hunger for blood of the modern despots?

Here are questions which few are capable of answering. Possible answers may be given, surface causes, reasons of immediate power. But no one will be willing to accept these as the true moving causes. For a continent to spring in a week's time from complete peace into almost universal war, with all the great and several of the small

Powers involved, is not to be explained by logic or embraced within the limits of a simple phrase.

If not all, certainly several of these nations had hatreds to be unchained, ambitions to be gratified, long-hidden goals to be put into action. They seemed to have been waiting an opportunity and it came when the anger of the Serbians at the seizure of Bosnia by Austria culminated in a mad act of assassination

ASSASSINATION OF THE AUSTRIAN CROWN PRINCE

The immediate cause, so far as apparent to us, of the war in question was the murder, on June 29, 1914, of the Austrian Crown Prince Francis Ferdinand and his wife, while on a visit to Sarajevo, the capital of Bosnia, the assassin being a Serbian student, supposed to have come for that purpose from Belgrade, the Serbian capital.

The inspiration for this dastardly act was the feeling of hostility towards Austria which was widely felt in Serbia. Bosnia was a part of the ancient kingdom of Serbia. The bulk of its people is of Slavic origin and speaks the Serbian language. Serbia was eager to regain it, as a possible outlet for a border on the Mediterranean Sea.

When, therefore, in 1908, Austria annexed Bosnia and Herzegovina, which had been under her military control since 1878, the indignation in Serbia was great. While it had died down in a measure in the subsequent years, the feeling of injury survived to the majority, and there is little reason to doubt that the assassination of Archduke Ferdinand was a result of this pervading sentiment.

In fact, the Austrian government was satisfied that the murder plot was hatched in Belgrade and held that Serbian officials were in some way concerned in it. The Serbian press gave some warrant for this, being openly boastful and defiant in its comments. When the Austrian consul-general at Belgrade dropped dead in the consulate the papers showed their satisfaction and hinted that he had been poisoned. This attitude of the press evidently was one of the reasons for the stringent demand made by Austria on July 23d, requiring apology and change of attitude from Serbia and asking for a reply by the hour of 6 P.M. on the 25th.

The demands were in part as follows:

1. An apology by the Serbian government in its official journal for all Pan-Serbian propaganda and for the participation of Serbian army officers in it, and warning all Serbians in the future to desist from anti-Austrian demonstrations.

2. That orders to this effect should be issued to the Serbian army.

3. That Serbia should dissolve all societies capable of conducting intrigues against Austria.

4. That Serbia should curb the activities of the Serbian press in regard to Austria.

5. That Austrian officials should be permitted to conduct an inquiry in Serbia independent of the Serbian government into the Sarajevo plot.

An answer to these demands was sent out at ten minutes before 6 0"clock on the 25th, in which Serbia accepted all demands except the last, which it did not deem "in accordance with international law and good neighborly relations." It asked that this demand should be submitted to The Hague Tribunal. The Austrian Minister at Belgrade, Baron Giesl von Gieslingen, refused to accept this reply and at once left the capital with the entire staff of the legation. The die was cast, as Austria probably intended that it should be.

AUSTRIA'S MOTIVE IN MAKING WAR

It had, in fact, become evident early in July that the military party in Austria was seeking to manufacture a popular demand for war, based on the assassination of the Archduke Ferdinand and his wife. Such was the indication of the tone of the Vienna newspapers, which appeared desirous of working up a sentiment hostile to Serbia. It may be doubted if the aged emperor was a party to this. Probably his assent was a forced one, due to the insistence of the war party and the public sentiment developed by it. That the murder of the Archduke was the real cause of the action of Austria can scarcely be accepted in view of Serbia's acceptance of Austria's rigid demands.

The actual cause was undoubtedly a deeper one, -- that of Austria's long-cherished purpose of gaining a foothold on the Aegean Sea, for which the possession of Serbia was necessary as a preliminary step. A plausible motive was needed, any pretext that would serve as a satisfactory excuse to Europe for hostile action and that could at the same time be utilized in developing Austrian indignation against the Serbians.

Such a motive came in the act of assassination and immediate use was made of it. The Austrian war party contended that the deed was planned at Belgrade, that it had been fomented by Serbian officials, and that these had supplied the murderer with explosives and aided in their transfer into Bosnia.

What evidence Austria possessed leading to this opinion we do not know. While it is not likely that there was any actual evidence, the case was one that called for investigation, and Austria was plainly within its rights in demanding such an inquiry and due punishment of every one found to be connected with the tragic deed.

But Austria went farther than this. It was willing to accept nothing less than a complete and humiliating submission on the part of Serbia. And the impression was widely entertained, whether with or without cause, that in this Austria was not acting alone but that it had the full support of Germany. That country also may be supposed to have had its ends to gain. What these were we shall consider later.

SERBIA ACCEPTS AUSTRIA'S DEMANDS

Characteristic as had been the demand of Austria, one which would never have been submitted to a Power of equal strength, Serbia accepted it, expressing itself as willing to comply with all the conditions imposed except that relating to the participation of Austrian officials in the inquiry, an explanation being asked on this point. If this reply should be deemed inadequate, Serbia stood ready to submit the question at issue to The Hague Peace Tribunal and to the Powers which had signed the declaration of 1909 relating to Bosnia and Herzegovina.

The subsequent action of Austria was significant. The Austrian Minister at Belgrade, as before stated, rejected it as unsatisfactory and immediately left the Serbian capital. He acted, in short, with a speed that indicated that he was acting under instructions. This was made very evident by what immediately followed. When news came on July 28th that war had been declared and active hostilities commenced, it was accompanied by the statement that Austria would not now be satisfied even with a full acceptance of her demands.

That the intention of this arrogant demand and what quickly followed was to force a war, no one can doubt. Serbia's nearly complete assent to the conditions imposed was declared to be not only unsatisfactory, but also "dishonorable," a word doubtless deliberately used. Evidently no door was to be left open for peace.

Chapter X
THE IRONIES OF HISTORY

It is one of the ironies of history that a people who once played a leading part in saving the Austrian capital from capture should come to be threatened by the armies of that capital. This takes us back to the era when Serbia, a powerful empire of those days, fell under the dominion of the conquering Turks, whose armies further overran Hungary and besieged Vienna.

Had this city been captured, all central Europe would have lain open to the barbarities of the Turks. In its defense the Serbians played a leading part, so great a one that we are told by a Hungarian historian, "It was the Serb Bacich who saved Vienna." But in 1914 Serbia was brought to the need of saving itself from Vienna.

WHAT AUSTRIA HAD TO GAIN

If it be asked what Austria had to gain by this act; what was her aim in forcing war upon a far weaker state; the answer is at hand. The Balkan States, of which Serbia is a prominent member, lie in a direct line between Europe and the Orient. A great power occupying the whole of the Balkan Peninsula would possess political advantages far beyond those enjoyed by Austria-Hungary.

It would be in a position giving it great influence over, if not strategic control of, the Suez Canal, the commerce of the Mediterranean, and a considerable all-rail route between Central Europe and the Far East. Salonika, on the Aegean Sea, now in Greek territory, is one of the finest harbors on the Mediterranean Sea. A railway through Serbia now connects this port with Austria and Germany.

In addition to this railway it is not unlikely that a canal may in the near future connect the Danube with the harbor of Salonika. If this project should be carried out, the commerce of the Danube and its tributary streams and canals, even that of central and western Germany, would be able to reach the Mediterranean without passing through the perilous Iron Gates of the Danube or being subjected to the delays and dangers incident to the long passage through the Black Sea and the Grecian Archipelago.

We can see in all this a powerful motive for Austria to seek to gain possession of Serbia, as a step towards possible future control of the whole Balkan Peninsula. The commercial and manufacturing interests of Austria-Hungary were growing, and mastership of such a route to the Mediterranean would mean an immense advantage to this ambitious empire.

Possession of northern Italy once gave her the advantage of an important outlet to the Mediterranean.

This, through events was lost to her. She apparently then sought to reach it by a more direct and open road, that leading through Salonika.

Such seem the reasons most likely to have been active in the Austrian assault upon Serbia. The murder of an Austrian archduke by an insignificant assassin gave no sufficient warrant for the act. The whole movement of events indicates that Austria was not seeking retribution for a crime but seizing upon a pretext for a predetermined purpose and couching her demands upon Serbia in terms which no self-respecting nation could accept without protest. Serbia was to be put in a position from which she could not escape and every door of retreat against the preventing war was closed against her.

But up to this time we've dealt with Austria and Serbia alone. What brought Germany, what brought France, what brought practically the whole of Europe into the struggle? What caused it to grow with startling suddenness from a minor into a major conflict, from a contest between a bulldog and a terrier into a battle between lions? What were the unseen conditions that, within little more than a week's time, induced all the leading nations of Europe to cast down the gage of battle and spring full-armed into the arena, bent upon a struggle which threatened to surpass any that the world had ever seen?

Certainly no trifling causes were here involved. Only great and far-reaching causes could have brought about such a catastrophe. All Europe appeared to be sitting, unknowingly or knowingly, upon a powder barrel which only needed some inconsequent hand to apply the match.

It seems incredible that the mere pulling of a trigger by a Serbian student and the slaughter of an archduke in the Bosnian capital could in a month's time have plunged all Europe into war. From small causes great events may arise!

HOW THE WAR BECAME CONTINENTAL

We cannot hope to point out the varied causes which were at work in this vast event. Very possibly the leading ones are unknown to us. Yet some of the important ones are evident and may be made.

Allusion has already been made to the general belief that the Emperor of Germany was deeply concerned in it, and that Austria would not have acted as it did without assurance of support, in fact without direct instigation, from some strong allied Power, and this Power is thought to have been Germany, acting in the person of its ambitious war lord, the dominating Kaiser.

It may be stated that all the Powers concerned have sought to disclaim responsibility. Thus Serbia called the world to witness that her answer to Austria was the limit of submission and conciliation. Austria, through her ambassador to the United States, solemnly declared that her assault upon Serbia was a measure of "self-defense." Russia explained her action as "benevolent intervention"!

Germany charged France with traitorous attack upon the unarmed border of the fatherland, and proclaimed a holy war for "the security of her territory." France and England, Belgium and Italy deplored the conflict and protested that they were innocent of offense. So far as all this is concerned the facts are generally held to point to Germany as the chief instigator of the war.

Russia, indeed, had made threatening movements toward Austria as a warning to her to desist from her threatened invasion of Serbia. Great Britain proposed mediation. Germany made no movement in the direction of preventing the war, but directed its attention to Russia, warning it to stop mobilization within twenty-four hours, and immediately afterward beginning a similar movement of mobilization in its own territory.

On August 1st Germany declared war against Russia, the first step towards making the contest a continental one. On the 2d, when France began mobilization, German forces moved against Russia and France simultaneously and invaded the neutral states of Luxembourg and Belgium. It was her persistence in the latter movement that brought Great Britain into the contest, as this country was pledged to support Belgian neutrality.

On August 4th, Great Britain sent an ultimatum to Germany to withdraw from the neutral territory which her troops had entered and demanded an answer by midnight. Germany declined to answer satisfactorily and at 11war was declared by Great Britain.

AN EDITORIAL OPINION

As regards the significance of these movements, in which Germany hurled declarations of war in rapid succession to east and west, and forced the issue of a continental war upon nations which had taken no decisive step, it may suffice to quote an editorial summing up of the situation as regards Germany, from the *Philadelphia North American* of August 7th: 1914--

"From these facts there is no escape. Leaving aside all questions of justice or political expediency, the aggressor throughout has been Germany. Austria's fury over the assassination of the heir to the throne was natural. But Serbia tendered full reparation.

So keen and conservative an authority as Rear Admiral Mahan declares that 'the aggressive insolence' of Austria's ultimatum 'and Serbia's concession of all demands except those too humiliating for national self-respect' show that behind Austria's assault was the instigation of Berlin. He adds: inference is irresistible that it was the pretext for a war already determined upon as soon as plausible occasion offered.'

"Circumstantial evidence, at least, places responsibility for the flinging of the first firebrand upon the government of the Kaiser. Now, who added fuel to the flames, until the great conflagration was under way?

"The next move was the Czar's. Fraternal sentiments of the Russian people for the Slavs in Serbia,' he says, led him to order partial mobilization, following Austria's invasion of Serbia. Instantly Germany protested, and within forty-eight hours sent an ultimatum demanding that Russia cease her preparations.

On the following day Germany began mobilizing, and twenty-four hours later declared war on Russia. Mobilization in France, necessitated by these events, was anticipated by Germany, which simultaneously flung forces into Russia, France, Luxembourg and Belgium.

"It was Germany's historic policy of "blood and iron" that fired Austria to attempt the crushing of Serbia. It was Germany that hurled an ultimatum, swiftly followed by an army, at Russia. It was Germany that struck first at the French frontier. It was Germany that trampled upon solemn treaty engagements by invading the neutral states of Luxembourg and Belgium. And it was Germany that, in answer to England's demand that the neutrality of Belgium be protected, declared war against Great Britain.

"Regardless, therefore, of questions of right and wrong, it is undeniable that in each succeeding crisis Germany has taken the aggressive. In so doing she has been inspired by a supreme confidence in her military might. But she has less reason to be proud of her diplomacy. The splendid audacity of her moves cannot obscure the fact that in making the case upon which she will be judged she has been outmaneuvered by the deliberation of Russia, the forbearance of France and the patience of Great Britain. She has assumed the role of international autocrat, while giving her foes the advantage of prosecuting a patriotic war of defense.

"Particularly is this true touching the violation of neutral territory. For nearly half a century the duchy of Luxembourg has been considered a 'perpetually neutral state,' under solemn guarantee of Austria, Great Britain, Germany and Russia. Since 1830, when Belgium seceded from the Netherlands, it, too, has been held 'an independent and perpetually neutral state,' that status being solemnly declared in a convention signed by Great Britain, France, Russia, Austria and Prussia. Yet the first war move of Germany was to overrun these countries, seize their railroads, bombard their cities and lay waste their territories.

"For forty years Germany has been the exemplar of a progressive civilization. In spite of her adherence to inflated militarism, she has put the whole world in her debt by her inspiring industrial and scientific achievements. Her people have taught mankind lessons of incalculable value, and her sons have enriched far distant lands with their genius. Not the least of the catastrophes inflicted by this inhuman war is that an unbridled autocracy has brought against the great German empire an indictment for arrogant assault upon the peace of nations and the security of human institutions."

IS THE KAISER RESPONSIBLE?

How much reliance is to be placed on the foregoing newspaper opinion, and on the prevailing sentiment holding Kaiser Wilhelm responsible for flinging the war bomb that disrupted the ranks of peace, no one can say. Every one naturally looked for the fomenter of this frightful international conflict and was disposed to place the blame on the basis of rumor and personal feeling.

On the other hand each nation concerned has vigorously disclaimed responsibility for the cataclysm. Austria – very meekly - claimed that Serbia precipitated the conflict. Germany blamed it upon Russia and France, the former from Slavic race sentiment, the latter from enmity that had existed since the loss of Alsace and Lorraine in 1870.

They, on the contrary, laid all the blame upon Germany. In the case of England alone we have a clear vista. The obligation of the island kingdom to maintain the neutral position of Belgium and the utter disregard of this neutrality by Germany forced her to take part and throw her armies into the field for the preservation of her international obligations.

Many opinions were given, many views advanced.

One of these, from Robert C. Long, a war correspondent of note, laid the total responsibility upon Austria, which, he said, plunged Europe into war in disregard of the Kaiser, who vigorously sought to prevent the outbreak, even threatening his ally in his efforts to preserve peace. In his view, "All the blood-guiltiness in this war will rest upon two Powers, Austria and Russia. It rests on Austria for her undue harshness to Serbia and on Russia for its dishonesty in secretly mobilizing its entire army at a time when it was imploring the Kaiser to intervene for peace, and when the Kaiser was working for peace with every prospect of success."

We have quoted one editorial opinion holding Germany wholly responsible. Here is another, from *The New York Times*, which, with a fair degree of justice, distributes the responsibility among all the warring nations of Europe:

"Germany is not responsible; Russia is not responsible, or Austria, or France, or England. The pillars of civilization are undermined and human aspirations bludgeoned down by no Power, but by all Powers; by no autocrats, but by all autocrats; not because this one or that has erred or dared or dreamed or swaggered, but because all, in a mad stampede for

armament, trade and territory, have sowed swords and guns, nourished harvests of death-dealing crops, made ready the way.

"For what reason other than war have billions in bonds and taxes been clamped on the backs of all Europe? None sought to evade war; each sought to be prepared to triumph when it came. At most some chancelleries whispered for delay, postponement; they knew the clash" For what reason other than war have billions in bonds and taxes to be inevitable; if not today, tomorrow. Avoid war!

What else have they lived for, what else prepared for, what else have they inculcated in the mind of youth than the sureness of the conflict and the great glory of offering themselves to this Moloch in sacrifice?

"No Power involved can cover up the stain. It is indelible, the sin of all Europe. It could have been prevented by common agreement. There was no wish to prevent it. Munitions manufacturers were not alone in urging the race to destruction, physical and financial. The leaders were for it. It was policy. A boiling pot will boil, a nurtured seed will grow. There was no escape from the avowed goal. A slow drift to the inevitable, a thunderbolt forged the awful push toward the vortex! What men and nations want they get."

ENRIGHT
HAY
"The First Three!"
Give till it Hurts
- they gave till they
died
War Fund
Week
One Hundred
Million Dollars

Chapter XI
GERMANY'S STAKE IN THE WAR

What had Germany to gain in the war in the instigation of which she is charged with being so deeply involved? Territorial aggrandizement may have been one of her purposes. Belgium and Holland lay between her and the open Atlantic, and the possession of these countries, with their splendid ports, would pay her well for a reasonable degree of risk and cost.

The invasion of Belgium as her first move in the war game may have had an ulterior purpose in the acquisition of that country, one likely to be as distasteful to France as the taking over of Alsace-Lorraine. Perhaps the neutral position taken by Holland, with her seeming inclination in favor of Germany, may have had more than racial relations behind it. Considerations of ultimate safety from annexation may have had its share in this attitude of neutrality.

The general impression has been that Germany went to war with the purpose of establishing beyond question her political and military supremacy on the European continent. Military despotism in Germany was the decisive factor in making inevitable the general war. The Emperor of Germany stood as the incarnation and exponent of the Prussian policy of military autocracy.

He had ruled all German States in unwavering obedience to the militarist maxim: "In times of peace prepare for war." He had used to the full his autocratic power in building up the German Empire and in making it not only a marvel of industrial efficiency, but also a stupendous military machine. In this effort he had burdened the people of Germany with an ever-increasing war budget.

The limit in this direction was reached with the war budget of the year 1912 when the revenues of the princes and of all citizens of wealth were specially taxed. No new sources of revenue remained. A crisis had come.

That crisis, as sometimes claimed, was not any menace from Britain or any fear of the British power. It was rather the very real and very rapidly rising menace of the new great Slav power on Germany's border, including, as it did, the Russian Empire and the entire line of Slav countries that encircled Germanic Austria from the Adriatic to Bohemia. These Slav peoples are separated from the governing Teutonic race in the Austrian Empire by the gulfs of blood, language, and religion. And in Europe the Slav population very largely outnumbers the Teutonic population and is growing much more rapidly.

Recent events, especially in the Balkan wars, had made it plain, not to the German Emperor alone, but to all the world, that the growth into an organized power of more than two hundred millions of Slav peoples along nearly three thousand miles of international frontier was a menace to the preservation of Teutonic supremacy in Europe.

That Teutonic supremacy was based on the sword. The German Emperor's appeal was to "My sword." But when the new sword of the united Slav power was allowed to be unsheathed, German supremacy was threatened on its own ground and by the weapon of its own choosing.

However all this be, and it must be admitted that it is to a degree speculative, there were in 1914 conditions existing that appeared to render the time a suitable one for the seemingly inevitable continental war. Revelations pointing to defects in the French army, deficiencies of equipment and weaknesses in artillery, had been made in the French Parliament.

The debate that occurred was fully dwelt upon in the German papers. And on July 16th the organ of Berlin radicalism, the VOSSICHE ZEITUNG, published a leading article to show that Russia was not prepared for war, and never had been. As for France, it said: "A Gallic cock with a lame wing is not the ideal set up by the Russians. And when the Russian eagle boasts of being in the best of health who is to believe him? Why should the French place greater confidence in the inveterate Russian disorganization than in their own defective organization?"

As regards the Kaiser's own estimate of his preparedness for war, and the views of national polity he entertained, we shall let him speak for himself in the following extracts from former utterances:

"We will be everywhere victorious even if we are surrounded by enemies on all sides and even if we have to fight superior numbers, for our most powerful ally is God above, who, since the time of the Great Elector and Great King, has always been on our side." - At Berlin, March 29, 1901.

"I vowed never to strike for world mastery. The world empire that I then dreamed of was to create for the German empire on all sides the most absolute confidence as a quiet, honest and peaceable neighbor. I have vowed that if ever the time came when history should speak of a German world power or a Hohenzollern world power this should not be based on conquest, but come through a mutual striving of nations after a common purpose.

"After much has been done internally in a military way, the next thing must be the arming ourselves at sea. Every German battleship is a new guarantee for the peace of the world. We are the salt of the earth, but must prove worthy of being so. Therefore, our youth must learn to deny what is not good for them.

"With all my heart I hope that golden peace will continue to be present with us." - At Bremen, March 22, 1905.

"My final and last care is for my fighting forces on land and sea. May God grant that war may not come, but should the cloud descend, I am firmly convinced that the army will acquit itself as it did so nobly thirty-five years ago." - At Berlin, February 25, 1906.

In the early days of the reign of William II war was prominent in his utterances. He was the War Lord in full feather, and the world at that time looked with dread upon this new and somewhat blatant apostle of militarism. Yet year after year passed until the toll of almost three decades was achieved, without his drawing the sword, and the world began to regard him as an apostle of peace, a wise and capable ruler who could gain his ends without the shedding of blood. What are we to believe now?

Had he been wearing a mast for all these years, biding his time, hiding from view a deeply cherished purpose? Or did he really believe that a mission awaited him, that regeneration of the world through the path of the battle-field was his duty, and that by the aid of a successful war he could inaugurate a safer and sounder era of peace?

We throw out these ideas as suggestions only. What the Kaiser purposed, what deep-laid schemes of international policy he entertained, will, perhaps, never be known. But if he was really responsible for the Great War, as he was so widely accused of being, the responsibility he assumed was an awful one. If he was not responsible, as he declared and as some who claim to have been behind the scenes maintain, the world will be ready to absolve him when his innocence has been made evident.

Chapter XII
WHY RUSSIA ENTERED THE FIELD

In this survey of the causes of the Great War under consideration the position of Russia comes next. That country was the first to follow Austria and begin the threatening work of mobilization. Germany's first open participation consisted in a warming to Russia that this work must cease. Only when her warning was disregarded did Germany begin mobilization and declare war.

All this was the work of a very few days, but in this era of active military preparedness it needs only days, only hours in some instances, to change from a state of peace into a state of war and hurl great armed hosts against the borders of hostile nations.

The general impression was that it was the Slavic race sentiment that inspired Russia's quick action. Serbia, a country of Slavs, brothers in race to a large section of the people of Russia, was threatened with national annihilation and her great kinsman sprang to her rescue, determined that she should not be absorbed by her land-hungry neighbor. This seemed to many a sufficient cause for Russia's action.

Not many years before, when Austria annexed her wards, Bosnia and Herzegovina, both Slavic countries, Russia protested against the act. She would doubtless have done more than protest but for her financial and military weakness arising from the then recent Russo-Japanese War.

In 1914 she was much stronger in both these elements of national power and lost not a day in preparing to march to Serbia's aid. But was this the whole, or indeed the chief, moving impulse in Russia's action? Was she so eager an advocate of Pan-Slavism as such a fact would indicate? Had she not some other purpose in view, some fish of her own to fry, some object of moment to obtain?

Many thought so. They were not willing to credit the Russian bear with an act of pure international benevolence. Wars of pure charity are rarely among the virtuous acts of nations. As it had been suggested, that Germany saw in the war a possible opportunity to gain a frontier on the Atlantic; so it was hinted that Russia had in mind gaining a similar its own frontier on the Mediterranean.

Time and again she had sought to wring Constantinople from the hands of the Turks. In 1877 she was on the point of achieving this purpose when she was halted and turned back by the Congress of Berlin and the bellicose attitude of the nations that stood behind it.

Here was another and seemingly a much better opportunity. The Balkan War had almost accomplished the conquest of the great Turkish capital and left Turkey in a state of serious weakness. If Europe should be thrown into the throes of a general war, in which every nation would have its own interests to care for, Russia's opportunity to seize upon the prize for which she had so long sought was an excellent one, and there being no one in a position to say her nay.

To Russia the possession of Constantinople was like the possession of a new world, and this may well have been her secret motive in springing without hesitation into the war. Her long-sought prize hung temptingly within reach of her hand, the European counterpart of the "Monroe Doctrine" could not now be evoked to stay her grasp, and it seems highly probable that in this may have laid the chief cause of Russia's participation in the war.

FRANCE'S HATRED OF GERMANY

The Republic of France was less hasty than Russia and Germany in issuing a declaration of war. Yet there, too, the order of mobilization was quickly issued and French troops were on the march toward the German border before Germany had taken a similar step.

France had not forgotten her humiliation in 1870. So far was she from forgetting it that she cherished a vivid recollection of what she had lost and an equally vivid enmity towards Germany in consequence. Enmity is hardly the word. Hatred better fits the feeling entertained. And this was kept vitally alive by the fact that Alsace and Lorraine, two of her former provinces, still possessing a considerable French population, were now held as part of the dominions of her enemy.

The sore rankled and hope of retribution lay deep in the heart of the French. Here seemed an opportunity to achieve this long-cherished purpose, and we may reasonably believe that the possibility of regaining this lost territory made France eager to take part in the coming war. She had been despoiled by Germany, a valued portion of her territory had been wrested from her grasp, a promising chance of regaining it lay before her. She had the men; she had the arms; she had a military organization vastly superior to that of 1870; she had the memory of her former triumphs over the now allied nations of Austria and Germany; she had her obligations to aid Russia as a further inducement.

The causes of her taking part in the war are apparent, especially in view of the fact that in a very brief interval after her declaration her troops had crossed the border and were marching gaily into Alsace, winning battles and occupying towns as they advanced.

Chapter XIII
GREAT BRITAIN AND ITALY

We have suggested that in the case alike of Austria, Russia, Germany and France the hope of gaining valuable acquisitions of territory was entertained. In the case of France, despising Germany was an added motive, the territory she sought being land of which she had been formerly robbed of.

These purposes of changing the map of Europe did not apply to or influence Great Britain. That country had no territory to gain and no great military organization to exercise. She possessed the most powerful navy of any country in the world, but she was moved by no desire of showing her strength upon the sea. There was no reason, so far as any special advantage to herself was concerned, for her taking part in the war, and her first step was a generous effort to mediate between the Powers in arms.

Only when Belgium - a small nation that was in a sense under the guardianship of Great Britain, so far as its nationality and neutrality were concerned - was invaded by Germany without warning, did Britain feel it incumbent upon her to come to its aid. This may not have been entirely an act of benevolence. There was a probability that Germany, once in control of Belgium, could not readily let go. She might add it to her empire, a fact likely to seriously affect British sea-power.

However this may be, Great Britain lost no time after the invasion in becoming a party to the continental war, sending her fleet abroad and enlisting troops for service in the aid of her allies--France and Belgium.

Italy, a member of the Triple Alliance, the other members of which were Germany and Austria, was the only one of the great Powers that held back. She had absolutely nothing to gain by taking part in the war, while her late large expenses in the conquest of Tripoli had seriously depleted her war chest. As regards her alliance with Germany and Austria, it put her under no obligation to come to their aid in an offensive war. Her obligation was restricted to aid in case they were attacked, and she justly held that no such condition existed. As a result, Germany and Austria found themselves at war with the three powerful members of the Triple Entente, while Italy, the third member of the Triple Alliance, declined to draw the sword.

The defection of Italy was a serious loss to the power of the allies, so much so that Emperor William threatened her with war if she failed to fulfill her assumed obligations. This threat Italy quietly ignored. She gave indications, in fact, that her sympathies were with the opposite party. Thus Germany and Austria found themselves pitted against three great Powers and a possible fourth, with the addition of the two small nations of Serbia and Belgium.

And the latter were not to be despised as of negligible importance. Serbia quickly showed an ability to check the forward movements of Austria, while Belgium, without aid, long held a powerful German army at bay, defending the city and fortresses of Liege with a boldness and success that called forth the admiring acclamations of the world.

THE TRIPLE ALLIANCE AND TRIPLE ENTENTE

This review of causes and motives may be supplemented by a brief statement of what is meant by the Triple Alliance and Triple Entente, terms which come into common prominence in discussing European politics.

They indicate the division of Europe, so far as its greater Powers are concerned, into two fully or partially allied bodies, the former consisting of Germany, Austria and Italy, the latter of Great Britain, France and Russia. These organizations are of comparatively recent date.

The Alliance began in 1879 in a compact between Germany and Austria, a Dual Alliance, which was converted into a Triple one in 1883, Italy then, through the influence of Bismarck, joining the alliance. In this compact Austria and Germany pledged themselves to mutual assistance if attacked by Russia; Italy and Germany to the same if attacked by France.

The Triple Entente - or Understanding - arose from a Dual Alliance between France and Russia, formed in 1887, an informal understanding between Britain and France in 1904 and a similar understanding between Britain and Russia in 1907. Its purpose, as formed by Edward VII, was to balance the Triple Alliance and thus convert Europe into two great military camps. When organized there seemed little probability of its being called into activity for many years.

Chapter XIV

THE SUPREME CRIME AGAINST CIVILIZATION: THE TRAGIC DESTRUCTION OF THE LUSITANIA--

NO THINKING man expects to have war without the horrors and atrocities which accompany it. That "war is hell" is as true now as when General Sherman so pronounced it. It seems, indeed, to be truer today. And yet we have always thought — perhaps because we hoped — that there was a limit at which even war, with all its lust of blood, with all its passion of hatred, with all its devilish zest for efficiency in the destruction of human life, would stop.

Now we know that there is no limit at which the makers of war, in their frenzy to pile horror on horror, and atrocity on atrocity, will stop. We have seen nations despoiled and raped because they resisted an invader, and we said that was war.

But now out of the sun-lit waves has come a venomous instrument of destruction, and without warning, without respite for escape, has sent headlong to the bottom of the everlasting sea more than a thousand unarmed, unresisting, peace-bent men, women and children — even babes in arms.

So the *Lusitania* was sunk. It may be war, but it is something incalculably more sobering than merely that. It is the difference between assassination and massacre. It is war's supreme crime against civilization.

AN UNPRECEDENTED CRIME AGAINST HUMANITY

The horror of the deadly assault on the *Lusitania* does not lessen as the first shock of the disaster recedes into the past. The world is aghast. It had not taken the German threat at full value; it did not believe that any civilized nation would be so wanton in its lust and passion of war as to count a thousand non- combatant lives a mere unfortunate incident of the carnage.

Nothing that can be said in mitigation of the destruction of the *Lusitania* can alter the fact that an outrage unknown heretofore in the warfare of civilized nations has been committed. Regardless of the technicalities which may be offered as a defense in international law, there are rights which must be asserted, must be defended and maintained. If international law can be torn to shreds and converted into scrap paper to serve the necessities of war, its obstructive letter can be disregarded when it is necessary to serve the rights of humanity.

CRIME AGAINST CIVILIZATION

THE *Lusitania*: built for safety--the irony of the situation lies in the fact that from the ghastly experience of great marine disasters the *Lusitania* was evolved as a vessel that was "safe." No such calamity as the attack of a torpedo was foreseen by the builders of the giant ship, and yet, even after the outbreak of the European war, and when upon the eve of her last voyage the warning came that an attempt would be made to torpedo the *Lusitania,* her owners confidently assured the world that the ship was safe because her great speed would enable her to outstrip any submarine ever built.

Limitation of language makes adequate word description of this mammoth Cunarder impossible. The following figures show its immense dimensions:

Length, 790 feet; breadth, 88 feet; depth, to boat deck, SO feet; draught, fully loaded, 37 feet, 6 inches; displacement on load line, 45,000 tons; height to top of funnels, 155 feet; height to mastheads, 216 feet.

The hull below draught line was divided into 175 water-tight compartments, which made it — so the owners claimed — "unsinkable."

With complete safety device equipment, including wireless telegraph, Mundy-Gray improved method of submarine signaling, and with officers and crew all trained and reliable men, the *Lusitania* was acclaimed as being unexcelled from a standpoint of safety, as in all other respects.

Size, however, was its least remarkable feature. The ship was propelled by four screws rotated by turbine engines of 68,000 horsepower, capable of developing a sea speed of more than twenty-five knots per hour regardless of weather conditions, and of maintaining without driving a schedule with the regularity of a railroad train, and thus establishing its right to the title of "the fastest ocean greyhound."

Germany's announced intention to sink the vessel on Saturday May 1, 1915, the day on which the Cunard liner *Lusitania,* carrying 2,000 passengers and crew, sailed from New York for Liverpool, the following advertisement, over the name of the Imperial German Embassy, was published in the papers---of the United States--

NOTICE!

TRAVELERS intending to embark on the Atlantic voyage are reminded that a state of war exists between Germany and her allies and Great Britain and her allies; that the zone of war includes the waters adjacent to the British Isles; that, in accordance with formal notice given by the Imperial German Government, vessels flying the

flag of Great Britain, or of any of her allies, are liable to destruction in those waters and that travelers sailing in the war zone on ships of Great Britain or her allies do so at their own risk. IMPERIAL GERMAN EMBASSY. Washington, D. C, April 22, 1915.

The advertisement was commented upon by the passengers of the *Lusitania*, but it did not cause any of them to cancel their bookings. No one took the matter seriously. It was not conceivable that even the German military lords could seriously plot so dastardly an attack on non-combatants.

When the attention of Captain W. T. Turner, commander of the *Lusitania*, was called to the warning, he laughed and said: "It doesn't seem as if they had scared many people from going on the ship by the looks of the passenger list."

Agents of the Cunard Line said there was no truth in reports that several prominent passengers had received anonymous telegrams warning them not to sail on the Lusitania. Charles T. Bowring, president of the St. George's Society, who was a passenger, said that it was a silly performance for the German Embassy to do.

Charles Klein, the American playwright, said he was going to devote his time on the voyage to thinking of his new play, "Potash and Perlmutter in Society," and would not have time to worry about trifles. Alfred G. Vanderbilt was one of the last to go on board.

Elbert Hubbard, publisher of the Philistine, who sailed with his wife, said he believed the German Emperor had ordered the advertisement to be placed in the newspapers, and added jokingly that if he was on board the liner when she was torpedoed, he would be able to do the Kaiser justice in the Philistine.

The early days of the voyage were unmarked by incidents other than those which have interested ocean passengers on countless previous trips, and little apprehension was felt by those on the *Lusitania* of the fate which lay ahead of the vessel.

The ship was proceeding at a moderate speed, on Friday, May 7, when she passed Fastnet Light, off Cape Clear, the extreme southwesterly point of Ireland that is first sighted by east-bound liners. Captain Turner was on the bridge, with his staff captain and other officers, maintaining a close lookout. Fastnet left behind, the *Lusitania*'s course was brought closer to shore, probably within twelve miles of the rock- bound coast.

The liner's speed increased as danger neared. Her speed was also increased to twenty knots or more, according to the more observant passengers, and some declare that she worked a sort of zigzag course, plainly ready to shift her helm whenever danger should appear. Captain Turner, it is known, was watching closely for any evidence of submarines.

One of the passengers, Dr. Daniel Moore, of Yankton, S. D., declared that before he went downstairs to luncheon shortly after one o'clock he and others with him noticed, through a pair of marine glasses, a curious object in the sea, possibly two miles or more away. What it was he could not determine, but he jokingly referred to it later at luncheon as a submarine.

While the first cabin passengers were chatting over their coffee cups they felt the ship give a great leap forward. Full speed ahead had suddenly been signaled from the bridge. This was a few minutes after two o'clock, and just about the time that Ellison Myers, of Stratford, Ontario, a boy on his way to join the British Navy, noticed the periscope of a submarine about a mile away to starboard. Myers and his companions saw Captain Turner hurriedly give orders to the helmsman and ring for full speed to the engine room.

The Lusitania began to swerve to starboard, heading for the submarine, but before she could really answer her helm a torpedo was flashing through the water toward her at express speed. Myers and his companions, like many others of the passengers, saw the white wake of the torpedo and its metal casing gleaming in the bright sunlight. The weather was ideal, calm winds and a clear sky making the surface of the ocean as beautiful and smooth as could be wished by any traveler.

The submarine's periscope dipped under surface, the torpedo came on, aimed apparently at the bow of the ship, but nicely calculated to hit her amidships. Before its wake was seen the periscope of the submarine had vanished beneath the surface.

In far less time than it takes to tell, the torpedo had crashed into the *Lusitania*'s starboard side, just abaft the first funnel, and exploded with a dull boom in the forward stoke-hole. Captain Turner at once ordered the helm put over and the prow of the ship headed for land, in the hope that she might strike shallow water while still under way. The lifeboats were ordered out, and the signals calling the boat crews to their stations were flashed everywhere through the vessel.

A mass grave for the innocent passengers of the *Lusitania.*

Several of the life-boats were already swung out, according to some survivors, there having been a lifesaving drill earlier in the day before the ship neared Fastnet Light.

Down in the dining saloon the passengers felt the ship reel from the shock of the explosion and many were hurled from their chairs. Before they could recover themselves, another explosion occurred. There is a difference of opinion as to the number of torpedoes fired. Some say there were two; others say only one torpedo struck the vessel, and that the second explosion was internal.

PASSENGERS OVERCOME BY POISONOUS FUMES

In any event, the passengers now realized their danger. The ship, torn almost apart, was filled with fumes and smoke, the decks were covered with debris that fell from the sky, and the great *Lusitania* began to list quickly to starboard. Before the passengers below decks could make their way above, the decks were beginning to slant ominously, and the air was filled with the cries of terrified men and women, some of them already injured by being hurled against the sides of the saloons.

Many passengers were stricken unconscious by the smoke and fumes from the exploding torpedoes. The stewards and stewardesses, recognizing the too evident signs of a sinking ship, rushed about urging and helping the passengers to put on life-belts, of which more than 3,000 were aboard.

The German U Boat that sank the Lusitania.

On the boat deck attempts were being made to lower the lifeboats, but several causes combined to impede the efforts of the crew in this direction. The port side of the vessel was already so far up that the lifeboats on that side were quite useless, and as the starboard boats were lowered from the plunging vessel — she was still speeding under headway, for all efforts to reverse the engines proved useless — the lifeboats swung back and forth, and when they struck the water were dragged along through the sea, making it almost impossible to get them away from the sinking ship.

American officials welcome Japanese Emperor to New York on board the *Lusitania*.

Chapter XV
BOAT CAPSIZES WITH WOMEN AND CHILDREN

The first life-boat that struck the water capsized with some sixty women and children aboard her, and all of these must have been drowned almost instantly. Ten more boats were lowered, the desperate expedient of cutting away the ropes being resorted to prevent them from being dragged along by the now speeding steamer.

A survivor of the Lusitania with his hand bandaged.

The great ship was sinking by the bow, foot by foot, and in ten minutes after the first explosion she w as already preparing to founder. Her stern rose high in the air, so that those in the boats that got away could see the whirring propellers, and even the boat deck was awash.

Captain Turner urged the men to be calm, to take care of the women and children, and megaphoned the passengers to seize life-belts, chairs — anything they could lay hands on to save themselves from drowning. There was never any question in the captain's mind that the ship was about to sink, and if, as reported, some of the stewards ran about advising the passengers not to take to the boats, that there was no danger of the vessel going down till she reached shore, it was done without his orders.

But many of the survivors have denied this, and declared that all the crew, officers, stewards and sailors, even the stokers, who dashed up from their flaming quarters below, showed the utmost bravery and calmness in the face of the disaster, and sought in every way to aid the panic-stricken passengers to get off the ship.

HUNDREDS JUMP INTO THE SEA

When it was seen that most of the lifeboats would be useless, hundreds of passengers donned life-belts and jumped into the sea. Others seized deck chairs, tubs, kegs, anything available, and hurled themselves into the water, clinging to these articles.

The first-cabin passengers fared worst, for the second and third-cabin travelers had long before finished their midday meal and were on deck when the torpedo struck. The first-cabin people on the D deck and in the balcony, at luncheon, were at a terrible disadvantage, and those who had already finished were in their staterooms resting or cleaning up preparing for the after luncheon day.

The confusion on the stairways became terrible, and the great number of little children, more than 150 of them under two years, a great many of them infants in arms, made the plight of the women still more desperate.

LUSITANIA GOES TO HER DOOM

After the life-boats had cut adrift it was plain that a few seconds would see the end of the great ship. With a great shiver she bent her bow down below the surface, and then her stern rose up, and with a horrible shriek the liner that had been the pride of the Cunard Line, plunged down in sixty fathoms of water.

The German U Boat that sunk the Lusitania is in the front row of U Boats in this photo, on right.

In the last few seconds the hundreds of women and men, a great many of them carrying children in their arms, leaped overboard, but hundreds of others, delaying the jump too long, were carried down in the suction that left a huge whirlpool swirling about the spot where the last of the vessel was seen.

Among these were Elbert Hubbard and his wife, Charles Frohman, who was crippled with rheumatism and unable to move quickly; Justice Miles Forman, Charles Klein, Alfred G. Vanderbilt and many others of the best-known Americans and Englishmen aboard.

Captain Turner stayed on the bridge as the ship went down, but before the last plunge he bade his staff officer and the helmsman, who were still with him, to save themselves. The helmsman leaped into the sea and was saved, but the staff officer would not desert his superior, and went down with the ship. He did not come to the surface again.

Captain Turner, however, a strong swimmer, rose after the eddying whirlpool had calmed down, and, seizing a couple of deck chairs, kept himself afloat for three hours. The master-at-arms of the *Lusitania* named Williams, who was looking for survivors in a boat after he had been picked up, saw the flash of the captain's gold-braided uniform, and rescued him, more dead than alive.

INTERVIEW WITH CAPTAIN TURNER

Despite the doubt as to whether two torpedoes exploded, or whether the first detonation caused the big liner's boilers to let go. Captain Turner stated that there was no doubt that at least two torpedoes reached the ship. "I am not certain whether the two explosions — and there were two — resulted from torpedoes, or whether one was a boiler explosion. I am sure, however, that I saw the first torpedo strike the vessel on her starboard side. I also saw a second torpedo apparently headed straight for the steamship's hull, directly below the suite occupied by

Alfred G. Vanderbilt."

American victims of the German U-Boat that torpedoed the unarmed passenger ship Lusitania.

When asked if the second explosion had been caused by the blowing up of ammunition stored in the liner's hull. Captain Turner said:

"No! If ammunition had exploded that would probably have torn the ship apart and the loss of life would have been much heavier than it was."

Captain Turner declared that, from the bridge, he saw the torpedo streaking toward the *Lusitania* and tried to change the ship's course to avoid the missile, but was unable to do so in time. The only thing left for him to do was to rush the liner ashore and beach her, and she was headed for the Irish coast when she foundered.

According to Captain Turner, the German submarine did not flee at once after torpedoing the liner. "While I was swimming about after the ship had disappeared, I saw the periscope of the submarine rise amidst the debris," said he. "Instead of offering any help the submarine immediately submerged herself and I saw nothing more of her. I did everything possible for my passengers. That was all I could do."

CHAPTER XVI
Heroes

EVERY great calamity produces its great heroes. Particularly this is true of marine disasters, where the opportunities of escape are limited, and where the heroism of the strong often impels them to stand back and give place to the weak. One cannot think of the *Titanic* disaster without remembering Major Archibald Butt, Colonel John Jacob Astor, Henry B. Harris, William T. Stead and others, nor of the sinking of the Empress of Ireland without calling to mind Dr. James F. Grant, the ship's surgeon; Sir Henry Seton-Karr, Lawrence Irving, H. R. O'Hara of Toronto, and the rest of the noble company of heroes.

So the destruction of the *Lusitania* brought uppermost in the breasts of many those qualities of fortitude and self-sacrifice which will forever mark them in the calendar of the world's martyrs.

THE HEROES OF THE LUSITANIA

ALFRED G. VANDERBILT GAVE LIFE FOR A WOMAN

Alfred G. Vanderbilt, at the Cunard pier in New York. He was one of the wealthiest men in the world and missed his trip on the Titanic. He died on the Lusitania.

Among the *Lusitania*'s heroes, one of the foremost was Alfred Gwynne Vanderbilt, one of America's wealthiest men. With everything to live for, Mr. Vanderbilt sacrificed his one chance for escape from the doomed Lusitania, in order that a woman might live. Details of the chivalry he displayed in those last moments when he tore off a his-lifebelt as he was about to leap into the sea, and strapped it around a young woman, were told by three of the survivors. Mr. Vanderbilt could not swim, and when he gave up his life-belt it was with the virtual certainty that he was surrendering his only chance for life.

Thomas Slidell, of New York, said he saw Mr. Vanderbilt on the deck as the *Lusitania* was sinking. He - was equipped with a life-belt and was climbing over the rail, when a young woman rushed onto the deck. Mr. Vanderbilt saw her as he stood poised to leap into the sea. Without hesitating a moment he jumped back to the deck, tore off the life-belt, strapped it around the young woman and dropped her overboard.

The *Lusitania* plunged under the waves a few minutes later and Mr. Vanderbilt was seen to be drawn into the vortex. Norman Ratcliffe, of Gillingham, Kent, and Wallace B. Phillips, a newspaper man, also saw Mr. Vanderbilt sink with the Lusitania. The coolness and heroism he showed were marvelous, they said.

An American victim of the Lusitania sinking is in crate being unloaded in New York.

Oliver P. Bernard, scenic artist at Covent Garden, saw Mr. Vanderbilt standing near the entrance to the grand saloon soon after the vessel was torpedoed. "He was the personification of sportsmanlike coolness Mr. Bernard said. "In his right hand was grasped what looked to me like a large purple leather jewel case. It may have belonged to Lady Mackworth, as Mr. Vanderbilt had been much in the company of the Thomas party during the trip and evidently had volunteered to do Lady Mackworth the service of saving her gems for her."

Another touching incident was told of Mr. Vanderbilt by Mrs. Stanley L. B. Lines, a Canadian, who said: "Mr. Vanderbilt will in the future be remembered as the 'children's hero.' I saw him standing outside the palm saloon on the starboard side, with Ronald Denit. He looked upon the scene before him, and then, turning to his valet, said:

"Find all the kiddies you can and bring them here." The servant rushed off and soon reappeared, herding a flock of little ones. Mr. Vanderbilt, catching a child under each arm, ran with them to a life-boat and dumped them in. He then threw in two more, and continued at his task until all the young ones were in the boat. Then he turned his attention to aiding the women into boats."

CHARLES FROHMAN DIED WITHOUT FEAR

"Why fear death? It is the most beautiful adventure in life," were the last words of Charles Frohman before he went down with the Lusitania, according to Miss Rita Jolivet, an American actress, with whom he talked calmly just before the end came. Miss Jolivet, who was among the survivors taken to Queenstown, said she and Mr. Frohman were standing on deck as the Lusitania heeled over. They decided not to trust themselves to lifeboats, although Mr. Frohman believed the ship was doomed. It was after reaching this decision that he declared he had no fear of death.

Dr. F. Warren Pearl, of New York, who was saved, with his wife and two of their four children, corroborated Miss Jolivet's statement, saying: "After the first shock, as I made my way to the deck, I saw Charles Frohman distributing life-belts. Mr. Frohman evidently did not expect to escape, as he said to a woman passenger, 'Why should we fear death? It is the greatest adventure man can have.' "

Sir James M. Barrie, in a tribute to Charles Frohman, published in the *London Daily Mail*, describes him as "the man who never broke his word.

"His companies were as children to him. He chided them as children, soothed them as children and forgave them and certainly loved them as children. He exulted in those who became great in that world, and gave them beautiful toys to play with; but great as was their devotion to him, it is not they who will miss him most, but rather the far greater number who never made a hit, but set off like all the rest, and fell by the way.

He was of so sympathetic a nature; he understood so well the dismalness to them of being failures, that he saw them as children, with their knuckles to their eyes, and then he sat back cross-legged on his chair, with his knuckles, as it were, to his eyes, and life had lost its flavor for him until he invented a scheme forgiving them another chance.

"Perhaps it is fitting that all those who only made for honest mirth and happiness should now go out of the world; because it is too wicked for them. It is strange to think that in America, Dernburg and Bernstorff, who we must believe were once good men, too, have an extra smile with their breakfast roll because they and theirs have drowned Charles Frohman."

SAVING THE BABIES

The presence of so many babies on board the *Lusitania* was due to the influx from Canada of the

English- born wives of Canadians at the battle front, who were coming to England to live with their own or their husband's parents during the war.

The pride of the Cunard line, the Lusitania arrives in New York.

No more pathetic loss has been recorded than that of F. G. Webster, a Toronto contractor, who was traveling second class with his wife, their six-year-old son Frederick and year-old tiny sons William and Henry. They reached the deck with others who were in the dining saloon when the torpedo struck. Webster took his son by the hand and darted away to bring life-belts. When he returned his wife and babies were not to be seen, nor have they been since.

The Lusitania steaming into New York harbor.

W. Harkless, an assistant purser, busied himself helping others until the Lusitania was about to founder. Then, seeing a life-boat striking the water that was not overcrowded, he made a rush for it. The only person he encountered was little Barbara Anderson, of Bridgeport, Conn., who was standing alone, clinging to the rail. Gathering her up in his arms he leaped over the rail and into the boat, doing this without injuring the child.

Francis J. Luker, a British subject, who had worked six years in the United States as a postal clerk, and was going home to enlist, saved two babies. He found the little passengers, bereft of their mother, in the shelter of a deck-house. The *Lusitania* was nearing her last plunge. A life-boat was swaying to the water below. Grabbing the babies he ran to the rail and made a flying leap into the craft, and those babies did not leave his arms until they were set safely ashore hours later.

One woman, a passenger on the Lusitania, lost all three of her children in the disaster, and gave the bodies of two of them to the sea herself. When the ship went down she held up the three children in the water, shrieking for help. When rescued two were dead. Their room was required and the mother was brave enough to realize it. "Give them to me!" she shrieked. "Give them to me, my bonnie wee things. I will bury them. They are mine to bury as they were mine to keep."

With her form shaking with sorrow she took hold of each little one from the rescuers and reverently placed them in the water again and the people in the boat wept with her as she murmured a little sobbing prayer. Just as the rescuers were landing her third and only remaining child died.

TORONTO GIRL OF FOURTEEN PROVES HEROINE

Even the young girls and women on the *Lusitania* proved themselves heroines during the last few moments and met their fate calmly or rose to emergencies which called for great bravery and presence of mind.

Fourteen-year-old Kathleen Kaye was returning from Toronto, where she had been visiting relatives. With a merry smile on her lips and with a steady patter of reassurance, she aided the stewards who were filling one of the life-boats.

Soon after the girl took her own place in the boat one of the sailors fainted under the strain of the efforts to get the boat clear of the whirlpools that marked where the liner went down. Miss Kaye took the abandoned oar and rowed until the boat was out of danger. None among the survivors bore fewer signs of their terrible experiences than Miss Kaye, who spent most of her time comforting and assisting her sisters in misfortune.

HEROISM OF CAPTAIN TURNER AND HIS CREW

Ernest Cowper, a Toronto newspaper man, praised the work of the Lusitania's crew in their efforts to get the passengers into the boats. Mr. Cowper told of having observed the ship watches keeping a strict lookout for submarines as soon as the ship began to near the coast.

The last view of the Lusitania from the German U Boat that fired on her and murdered so many civilians would have been similar to this photo.

"The crew proceeded to get the passengers into boats in an orderly, prompt and efficient manner. Helen Smith, a child, begged me to save her. I placed her in a boat and saw her safely away. I got into one of the last boats to leave. "Some of the boats could not be launched, as the vessel was sinking. There were a large number of women and children in the second cabin. Forty children were less than a year old."

WOMAN RESCUED "WITH DEAD BABY AT HER BREAST

R. J. Timmis, of Gainesville, Tex., a cotton buyer, who was saved after he had given his life-belt to a woman steerage passenger who carried a baby, told of the loss of his friend, R. T. Moodie, also of Gainesville. Moodie could not swim, but he took off his lifebelt and put it on a woman who had a six- months-old child in her arms. Timmis tried to help Moodie, and they both clung to some wreckage for a while, but presently Moodie could hold out no longer and sank. Later Timmis was dragged into a boat which he helped to right — it had been overturned in the suction of the sinking vessel — one of the first persons he assisted into the boat was the steerage woman to whom he had given his belt. She still carried her baby at her breast, but it was dead from exposure.

HEROIC WIRELESS OPERATORS

Oliver P. Brainard told of the bravery of the wireless operators who stuck to their work of summoning help even after it was evident that only a few minutes could elapse before the vessel must go down. He said:

"The wireless operators were working the emergency outfit, the main installation having been put out of gear instantaneously after the torpedo exploded. They were still awaiting a reply and were sending out the S. O. S. call. "I looked out to sea and saw a man, undressed, floating quietly on his back in the water, evidently waiting to be picked up rather than to take the chance of getting away in a boat. He gave me an idea and I took off my jacket and waistcoat, put my money in my trousers pocket, unlaced my boots and then returned to the Marconi men.

"The assistant operator said, 'Hush! We are still hoping for an answer. We don't know yet whether the S. O. S. calls have been picked up or not.'

"At that moment the chief operator turned around, saying, ‘they’ve got it!'

"At that very second the emergency apparatus also broke down. The operator had left the room, but he dashed back and brought out a Kodak. He knelt on the deck, now listing at an angle of thirty- five degrees, and took a photograph looking forward.

"The assistant, a big, cheerful chap, lugged out the operator's swivel chair and offered it to me with a laugh, saying: 'Take a seat and make yourself comfortable.' He let go the chair and it careened down the deck and over into the sea."

F. J. Gauntlet, of New York and Washington, traveling in company with A. L. Hopkins, president of the Newport News Shipbuilding Company, and S. M. Knox, president of the New York Shipbuilding Company, of Philadelphia, unconsciously told the story of his own heroism. He said:

"I was lingering in the dining saloon chatting with friends when the first explosion occurred. Some of us went to our staterooms and put on life-belts. Going on deck we were informed that there was no danger, but the bow of the vessel was gradually sinking. The work of launching the boats was done in a few minutes. Fifty or sixty people entered the first boat. As it swung from the davits it fell

The Gardner brothers are escorted following surviving the sinking of the Lusitania.

suddenly and I think most of the occupants perished. The other boats were launched with the greatest difficulty.

"Swinging free from one of these as it descended, I grabbed what I supposed was a piece of wreckage. I found it to be a collapsible boat, however. I had great difficulty in getting it open, finally having to rip the canvas with my knife. Soon another passenger came alongside and entered the collapsible with me. We paddled around and between us we rescued thirty people from the water."

SAVED HIS WIFE AND HELPED IN RESCUE WORK

George A. Kessler, of New York, said: "A list to starboard had set in as we were climbing the stairs and it had so rapidly increased by the time we reached the deck that we were falling against the rail. I managed to get my wife onto the first-class deck and there three boats were being launched.

'I placed her in the third, kissed her good-by and saw the boat lowered safely. Then I turned to look for a life-belt for myself. The ship now started to go down. I fell into the water, and some kind soul threw me a lifebelt at the same time. Ten minutes later I found myself beside a raft on which there were some survivors, who pulled me onto it. We cruised around looking for others and managed to pick up a few, making up perhaps sixteen or seventeen persons who were on the raft.

In all directions were scattered persons struggling for their lives and the boats gave what help they could. We saved all the women and children we could"

W. G. E. Meyers, of Stratford, Ont., a lad of sixteen years, who was on his way to join the British navy as a cadet, told this story:

"I went below to get a life-belt and met a woman who was frenzied with fear. I tried to calm her and helped her into a boat. Then I saw a boat which was nearly swamped. I got into it with other men and baled it out. Then a crowd of men clambered into it and nearly swamped it again. We had got only two hundred yards away when the Lusitania sank, bow first. Many persons were, drawn down by the suction. Their shrieks were appalling. We had to pull hard to get away, and, as it was, we were almost dragged down. We saved all the women and children we could, but a great many of them went down."

H. Smethhurst, a steerage passenger, put his wife into a life-boat, and in spite of her urging refused to accompany her, saying the women and children must go first. After the boat with his wife in it had pulled away Smethhurst put on a life-belt, slipped down a rope into the water and floated until he was picked up.

The medal struck by Germany to commemorate the sinking of the Lusitania.

CHAPTER XVII
Survivor Stories

AMONG the stories of the Lusitania horror told by the survivors were a few that stand out from the rest for their clearness and vividness. One of the most interesting of these, notable for the prominence of the man who relates it as well as for its conciseness, was the description given by Samuel M. Knox, president of the New York Shipbuilding Company. Mr. Knox said:

"Shortly after two, while we were finishing luncheon in a calm sea, a heavy concussion was felt on the starboard side, throwing the vessel to port. She immediately swung back and proceeded to take on a hit to starboard, which rapidly increased.

Dr. Carl Elmer Foss was a survivor of the Lusitania disaster.

"The passengers quickly, but in good form, left the dining room, proceeding mostly to the A or the boat deck. There were preparations being made to launch the boats. Order among the passengers was well maintained, there being nothing approaching a panic.

Many of the passengers had gone to their staterooms and provided themselves with lifebelts. "The vessel reached an angle of about twenty-four degrees and at this point there seemed to be a cessation in the listing, the vessel maintaining this position for four or five minutes, when something apparently gave way, and the list started anew and increased rapidly until the end.

"The greater number of passengers were congregated on the high side of the ship, and when it became apparent that she was going to sink I made my way to the lower side, where there appeared to be several boats only partly filled and no passengers on that deck. At this juncture I found the outside of the boat deck practically even with the water and the ship was even farther down by the head.

COULD NOT LAUNCH BOATS

"I stepped into a boat and a sailor in charge then attempted to cast her off, but it was found that the boat-falls (ropes) had fouled the boat and she could not be released in the limited time available. I went overboard at once and attempted to get clear of the ship, which was coming over slowly. I was caught by one of the smokestacks and carried down a considerable distance before being released.

"On coming to the surface I floated about for a considerable time, when I was picked up by a life raft. This raft, with others, had floated free when the vessel sank, and had been picked up and taken charge of by Mr. Gauntlet, of Washington, and Mr. Lamiat, of Boston, who picked up thirty-two persons in all.

"It was equipped with oars, and we made our way to a fishing smack, about five miles distant, which took us on board, although it was already overloaded. We were

Mr. J. Lane and Miss B. Williams, both survived the sinking of the Lusitania.

finally taken off this boat by the Cunard tender Flying Fish and brought to Queenstown at 9.30."

Some of the passengers, notably David A. Thomas, told of panic- conditions on board the vessel before she sank, and one of the rescued declared that the loss of life was due to some extent to the assurances spread by the stewards among the passengers that there was no danger of the Lusitania sinking. But all were united in praising the courage and steadiness of the officers and crew of the ship.

SAYS SHIP SANK IN FIFTEEN MINUTES

Mr. Thomas, a Cardiff, Wales, coal magnate, who was rescued with his daughter, Lady Mackworth, said that not more than fifteen minutes elapsed between the first explosion and thc sinking of the ship. Lady Mackworth had put on her -preserver and went down with the Lusitania. When she arose to the surface, Mr. Thomas said, she was unconscious, and floated around in the tumbling sea for three and a half hours before she was picked up.

"As soon as the explosions occurred," said Mr. Thomas, "and the officers learned what had happened, the ship's course was directed toward the shore, with the idea of beaching her. Captain Turner remained upon the bridge until the ship went down, and he was swallowed up in the swirl that followed. He wore a lifebelt, which kept him afloat. He rose to the surface, and remained in the water for three hours before he was picked up by a lifeboat.

The Lusitania in 1914.

"During the last few minutes of the Lusitania she was a ship of panic and tumult. Excited men and terrified women ran shouting and screaming about the decks. Lost children cried shrilly. Officers and seamen rushed among the panic- stricken passengers, shouting orders and helping the women and children into lifeboats.

Women clung desperately to their husbands or knelt on the deck and prayed. Life-preservers were distributed among the passengers, who hastily donned them and flung themselves into the water.

SCREAMS INTENSIFY HORROR

"In their haste and excitement the seamen over-loaded one lifeboat and the davit ropes broke while it was being lowered, the occupants being thrown into the water. The screams of these terrified women and men intensified the fright of those still on the ship. Altogether I counted ten life-boats launched."

A German submarine was seen for an hour before the liner was sunk, according to Dr. Daniel Moore, of Yankton, S. D., who said: "About 1 p.m. we noticed that the Lusitania was steering a zigzag course. Land had been in sight for three hours, distinctly visible twelve miles away.

This man was described as a "cripple" who had been saved. Life belts were difficult to find in the confusion.

Looking through my glasses, I could see on the port side of the Lusitania, between us and land, what appeared to be a black, oblong object, with four dome-like projections. It was moving along parallel to us, more than two miles away. At times it slowed down and disappeared. But always it reappeared.

All this time the Lusitania was zigzagging along. Later the Lusitania kept a more even course, and we generally agreed then that it was a friendly submarine we were watching. We had seen no other vessels except one or two fishing boats.

"At 1:40 we sat down to luncheon in the second saloon. We talked of the curious object we had seen, but nobody seemed anxious or concerned. About two o'clock a muffled, drum-like noise sounded from the forward part of the Lusitania and she shivered and trembled. Almost immediately she began to list to starboard. She had been struck on the starboard side. Unless the first submarine seen had been speedy enough to make rings around the Lusitania, this torpedo must have come from a second submarine which had been lying hidden to starboard.

"We heard no sound of explosion. There was general excitement among the passengers at luncheon, but the women were soon quieted by assurances that there was no danger and that the Lusitania had merely struck a small mine. The passengers left the saloon in good order.

ON HUNT FOR THE LIFE-BELTS

"As I reached the deck above I had difficulty in walking owing to the tilt of the vessel. With most of the passengers I ran on to the promenade deck. There was no crushing. Although the deck was crowded; I looked over the side; but I could see no evidence of damage. I started to return to my cabin, but the list of the liner was so marked that I abandoned the idea and regained the deck. Looking over the starboard rail, I saw that the water was now only about twelve feet from the rail at one point. While searching for a lifebelt I came upon a stewardess struggling with a pile of lifebelts in a rack below deck and helped her put one on, afterward securing one for myself. I had tremendous difficulty in reaching the promenade deck again.

"The Lusitania now was on her side and sinking by the bow. I saw a woman clinging to the rail near where a boat was being lowered. I pushed her over the rail into the boat, afterward jumping down myself. The boat fell bodily into the sea, but kept afloat, although so heavily loaded that water was lapping in. We bailed with our hats, but could not keep pace with the water, and I realized we must soon sink.

"Seeing a keg, I threw it overboard and sprang after it. A young steward named Freeman also used the keg as a support. Looking back, I saw the boat I had left swamped. We clung to the keg for about an hour and a half and then were picked up by a raft on which were twenty persons, including two women.

We had oars and rowed toward land. At about four o'clock we were picked up by the patrol boat Brook. She took us aboard and then cruised out to where the Lusitania had gone down, picking up many survivors there, also taking aboard many from boats and rafts.

INJURED BOY SHOWS PLUCK

"A number of those picked up were injured, including a little boy, whose left thigh was broken. I improvised splints for him and set his leg. He was a plucky little chap, and was soon asking, 'Is there a funny paper aboard?'

"At the scene of the catastrophe the surface of the water had seemed dotted with bodies. Only a few lifeboats seemed to be doing good. Cries of 'Save us! Help!' gradually grew weaker from all sides. Finally low wailings made the heart sick. I saw many men die.

"There was no suction when the ship settled. It went down steadily. The lifeboats were not in order and they were not manned. Weighing all the fact soberly convinces me that it was only through the mercy of God that any one was saved. Are there any bounds to this modern vandalism?"

L. Tonner, a County Dublin man, and a stoker on the Lusitania, who was one of the survivors landed at Kinmle, said: "There must have been two submarines attacking the Lusitania. The first torpedoed us on the starboard side, and right through the engine room a few minutes afterward the Lusitania received a second torpedo on the port side. The Lusitania listed so heavily to starboard that it was impossible to lower the boats on the port side."

MANY CHILDREN DROWNED

G. D. Lane, a youthful but cool-headed second- cabin passenger, who was returning to Wales from New York, was in a life-boat which was capsized by the davits as the Lusitania heeled over.

"I was on the B deck," he said, "when I saw the wake of a torpedo. I hardly realized what it meant when the big ship seemed to stagger and almost immediately listed to starboard. I rushed to get a lifebelt, but stopped to help get children on the boat deck. The second cabin was a veritable nursery.

"Many youngsters must have drowned, but I had the satisfaction of seeing one boat get away filled with women and children. When the water reached the deck I saw another life-boat with a vacant seat, which I took, as no one else was in sight, but we were too late. The Lusitania reeled so suddenly our boat was swamped, but we righted it again.

"We now witnessed the most horrible scene of human futility it is possible to imagine. When the *Lusitania* had turned almost over she suddenly plunged bow foremost into the water, leaving her stern high in the air. People on the aft deck were fighting with wild desperation to retain a footing on the almost perpendicular deck while they fell over the slippery stern like crippled flies.

"Their cries and shrieks could be heard above the hiss of escaping steam and the crash of bursting boilers. Then the water mercifully closed over them and the big liner disappeared, leaving scarcely a ripple behind her.

"Twelve life-boats were all that were left of our floating home. In time which could be measured by seconds --swimmers, bodies and wreckage appeared in the space where she went down. I was almost exhausted by the work of rescue when taken aboard the trawler. It seems like a horrible dream now."

WOMEN RUSHED FOR THE BOATS

According to another American survivor, W. H. Brooks, "there was a scene of great confusion as women and children rushed for the boats which were launched with the greatest difficulty and danger, owing to the tilting of the ship. "I heard the captain order that no more boats be launched, so I leaped into the sea. After I reached the water there was another explosion which sent up a shower of wreckage."

THREATENED SEAMEN WITH REVOLVER

Isaac Lehmann, of New York, a first-cabin passenger, who described himself as being engaged in the Department of Government Supplies, said that after having witnessed an accident to one of the boats through the snapping of the ropes while it was being lowered, he ran into his cabin and seizing a revolver and a lifebelt, returned to the deck and mounted a collapsible boat and called to some of the crew to assist in launching it. One sailor, he said, replied that the captain's orders were that no boats were to be put out.

"I drew my revolver, which was loaded with ball cartridges," said Mr. Lehmann, "and shouted 'I'll shoot the first man v/ho refuses to assist in launching.' The boat was then lowered. At least sixty persons were in it. Unfortunately, the Lusitania lurched so badly that the boat repeatedly struck the side of the sinking ship, and I think at least twenty of its occupants were killed or injured.

"At that instant we heard an explosion on the right up forward, and within two minutes the liner disappeared. I was thrown clear of the wreckage, and went down twice, but the life-belt that I had on brought me up. I was in the water for four and a half hours.

Asked as to the probable speed of the Lusitania when she was struck by the torpedo, Mr. Lehmann said the boat was probably going at about sixteen or seventeen knots.

Juhan de Ayala, Consul General for Cuba at Liverpool, said that he was ill in his berth when the Lusitania was torpedoed. He was thrown against the partition of his berth by the explosion and suffered an injury to his head and had flesh torn off one of his legs. The boat Mr. de Ayala got into capsized and he was thrown into the water, but later he was picked up.

"Captain Turner," said Mr. de Ayala, "thought he could bring the crippled vessel into Queenstown, but she rapidly began to sink by the head.

"Her stern went up so high," Mr. de Ayala added, "that we could see all of her propellers, and she went down with a headlong plunge, volumes of steam hissing from her funnels."

RESCUED UNCONSCIOUS FROM THE WATER

The experience of two New York girls-- Miss Mary Barrett and Miss Kate MacDonald, rescued at the last minute, may be taken as typical of the experience of many others. Miss Barrett gives the following account of her experiences:

"We had gone into the second saloon and were just finishing lunch. I heard a sound something like the smashing of big dishes and then there came a second and louder crash. Miss MacDonald and I started to go upstairs, but we were thrown back by the crowd when the ship stopped. But we managed to get to the second deck, where we found sailors trying to lower boats.

"There was no panic and the ship's officers and crew went about their work quietly and steadily. I went to get two lifebelts, but a man standing by told us to remain where we were and he would fetch them for us. He brought us two belts and we put them on. By this time the ship was leaning right over to starboard and we were both thrown down. We managed to scramble to the side of the liner. "Near us I saw a rope attached to one of the lifeboats. I thought I could catch it, so we murmured a few words of prayer and then jumped into the water; I missed the rope, but floated about in the water for some time. I did not lose consciousness at first, but the water got into my eyes and mouth and I began to lose hope of ever seeing my friends again. I could not see anybody near me. Then I must have lost consciousness, for I remember nothing more until one of the Lusitania's life-boats came along. The crew was pulling on board another woman, who was unconscious, and they shouted to me, "You hold on a little longer!"

"After a time they lifted me out of the water. Then I remembered nothing more for a time. In the meantime our boat had picked up twenty others. It was getting late in the evening when we were transferred to a trawler and taken to Queenstown.

CHAPTER XVIII
Graphic Stories

PERCY ROGERS, assistant manager and secretary of the Canadian National Exhibition, who went to England in connection with the Toronto Fair, told a graphic story of his experiences after the *Lusitania* was struck. He undoubtedly owed his life to the fact that he was a good swimmer.

"It had been a splendid crossing," he said, "with a calm sea and fine weather contributing to a delightful trip. The *Lusitania* made nothing like her maximum pace. Her speed probably was about five hundred miles daily, which, as travelers know, is below her average.

"Early Friday morning we sighted the Irish coast. Then we entered a slight fog, and speed was reduced, but we soon came into a clear atmosphere again, and the pace of the boat increased. The morning passed and we went as usual down to lunch, although some were a little later than others in taking the meal. I should think it would be about ten minutes past two when I came from lunch. I immediately proceeded to my stateroom, close to the dining-room, to get a letter which I had written. While in there I heard a tremendous thud, and I came out immediately.

PASSENGERS WERE AGHAST

"There was no panic where I was, but the people were aghast. It was realized that the boat had been struck, apparently on the side nearest the land. The passengers hastened to the boat deck above. The lifeboats were hanging out, having been put into that position on the previous day. The *Lusitania* soon began to list badly with the result that the side on which I and several others were standing went up as the other side dropped. This seemed to cause difficulty in launching the boats, which seemed to get bound against the side of the liner.

It was impossible, of course, for me to see what was happening in other places, but among the group where I was stationed there was no panic. The order was given, 'Women and children first,' and was followed implicitly. The first lifeboat lowered with people at the spot where I stood smacked upon the water, and as it did so the stern of this life-boat seemed to part and the people were thrown into the sea. The other boats were lowered more successfully.

"We heard somebody say, 'Get out of the boats; there is no danger,' and some people actually did get out, but the directions were not generally acted upon. I entered a boat in which there were men, women and children, I should say between twenty and twenty-five. There were no other women or children standing on the liner where we were, at our position, I should think.

CHAPTER XIX
World Hears the Awful Story!

FROM THE lips of Captain Turner, of the *Lusitania*, and from several of the survivors the world has heard the story of the sudden appearance among the debris and the dead of the sunken liner, of the German submarine that had fired the torpedo which sent almost 1,200 non-combatants, hundreds of them helpless women and children, and among them more than a hundred American citizens, to their deaths. But it remained for the captain of the steamship *Etonian*, arriving at Boston on May 18, to add the crowning touches to the tragedy.

Captain William F. Wood, of the *Etonian*, specifically charged that two German submarines deliberately prevented him from going to the rescue of the *Lusitania's* passengers after he had received the liner's wireless S. 0. S. call, and when he was but forty miles or so away, and might have rendered great assistance to the hundreds of victims. Captain Wood charged further that two other ships, both within the same distance of the Lusitania when she sank, were warned off by submarines, and that when the nearest one, the *Narragansett*, bound for New York, persisted in the attempt to proceed to the rescue of the *Lusitania's* passengers, a submarine fired a torpedo at her, which missed the *Narragansett* by only a few feet.

STORY OF ETONIAN'S CAPTAIN

The *Etonian* is a freight-carrying steamship, owned by the Wilson-Furness-Leyland Lines, and under charter to the Cunard Line. She sailed from Liverpool on May 6.

Captain Wood's story, as he told it without embellishment and in the most positive terms, was as follows:

"We had left Liverpool without unusual incident, and it was two o'clock on the afternoon of Friday, May 7, that we received the S0S call from the *Lusitania*. Her wireless operator sent this message: 'We are ten miles south of Kinsale. Come at once.'

"I was then about forty-two miles from the position he gave me. Two other steamships were ahead of me, going in the same direction. They were the *Narragansett* and the *City of Exeter*. The *Narragansett* was closer to the *Lusitania*, and she answered the S0S call.

*'At 5 pm I observed the *City of Exeter* across our bow and she signaled, 'Have you heard anything of the disaster?' "At that very moment I saw the periscope of a submarine between the *Etonian* and the *City of Exeter*. The submarine was about a quarter of a mile directly ahead of us. She immediately dived as soon as she saw us coming for her. I distinctly saw the splash in the water caused by her submerging.

DODGED TWO SUBMARINES

"I signaled to the engine room for every available inch of speed, and there was a prompt response. Then we saw the submarine come up astern of us with the periscope in line afterward. I now ordered full speed ahead, and we left the submarine slowly behind. The periscope remained in sight about twenty minutes. Our speed was perhaps two miles an hour better than the submarine could do.

"No sooner had we lost sight of the submarine astern than I made out another on the starboard bow. This one was directly ahead and on the surface, not submerged. I star-boarded hard away from him, -- he swinging as we did. About eight minutes later he submerged. I continued at top speed for four hours, and saw no more of the submarines. It was the ship's speed that saved her. That's all.

Christmas mail being unloaded from the Lusitania.

"Both these submarines were long craft, and the second one had wireless masts. There is no question in my mind that these two submarines were acting in concert and were so placed as to torpedo any ship that might attempt to go to the rescue of the passengers of the *Lusitania*.

"As a matter of fact, the *Narragansett*, as soon as she heard the S0S call, went to the assistance of the *Lusitania*. One of the submarines discharged a torpedo at her and missed her by a few feet. The *Narragansett* then warned us not to attempt to go to the rescue of the *Lusitania,* and I got her wireless call while I was dodging the two submarines. You can see that three ships would have gone to the assistance of the *Lusitania* had it not been for the two submarines.

These German craft were, it seems to me, deliberately stationed off Old Head of Kinsale, at a point where all ships have got to pass, for the express purpose of preventing any assistance being given to the passengers of the *Lusitania*."

NARRAGANSETT DRIVEN OFF

That the British tank steamer *Narragansett*, one of the vessels that caught the distress signal of the *Lusitania*, was also driven off her rescue course by a torpedo from a submarine when she arrived within seven miles of the spot where the *Lusitania* went down, an hour and three-quarters after she caught the wireless call for help, was alleged by the officers of the tanker, which arrived at Bayonne, N. J., on the same day that the *Etonian* reached Boston.

The story told by the officers of the *Narragansett* corroborated the statements made by officers of the *Etonian.* They said that submarines were apparently scouting the sea to drive back rescue vessels when the *Lusitania* fell a victim to another undersea craft. The Lusitania's call for help was received by the *Narragansett* at two o'clock on the afternoon of May 7, according to wireless operator Talbot Smith, who said the message read: "Strong list. Come quick."

When the *Narragansett* received the message she was thirty-five miles southeast of the *Lusitania*, having sailed from Liverpool the preceding afternoon at five o'clock for Bayonne. The message was delivered quickly to Captain Charles Harwood, and he ordered the vessel to put on full steam and increase her speed from eleven to fourteen knots. The *Narragansett* changed her course and started in the direction of the sinking ship.

TORPEDO FIRED AT NARRAGANSETT

Second Officer John Letts, who was on the bridge, said he sighted the periscope of a submarine at 3.35 o'clock, and almost at the same instant he saw a torpedo shooting through the water. The torpedo, according to the second officer, was traveling at great speed.

It shot past the *Narragansett,* missing the stern by hardly thirty feet, and disappeared. The periscope of the submarine went out of sight at the same time, but the captain of the *Narragansett* decided not to take any chance, changed the course of his vessel so that the stern pointed directly toward the spot where the periscope was last sighted, and, after steering straight ahead for some distance, followed a somewhat zigzag course until he was out of the immediate submarine territories.

Captain Harwood abandoned all thought of the *Lusitania's* call for help, because he thought it was a decoy message sent out to trap the *Narragansett* into the submarine's path.

"My opinion," said Second Officer Letts, "is that submarines were scattered around that territory to prevent any vessel that received the S. O. S. call of the *Lusitania* from going to her assistance."

When attacked by the submarine the *Narragansett* had out her log, according to Second Officer Letts, and the torpedo passed under the line to which it was attached. The torpedo was fired from the submarine when the undersea boat was within two hundred yards. The *Narragansett* then turned back and had not sighted the wreck of the *Lusitania*, and her officers, who were led to believe the SOS was a decoy, did not learn of the sinking of the Cunarder until the following morning at two o'clock.

The *Narragansett*, under charter to the Standard Oil Company, is one of the largest tank steamships afloat. She is 540 feet long, has a sixty-foot beam, and 12,500 tons displacement.

The *Narragansett* was sailing to answer the SOS of the *Lusitania* when a U Boat fired a torpedo at her, turning her away from picking up survivors. She was later sunk by a U Boat during WWI.

CHAPTER XX

TESTIMONY OF CORONER HORGAN

ONE OF the first official acts with reference to the loss of the *Lusitania* was the impaneling, on May 10, of a coroner's jury at Queenstown to fix the responsibility for the death of the passengers whose bodies were recovered and taken to that place. The inquest was conducted by Coroner John Horgan. The coroner's proceedings were comparatively brief, and were concluded with the return of the following verdict of the jury:

"The crime of wholesale murder"

"We find that the deceased met death from prolonged immersion and exhaustion in the sea eight miles south-southwest of Old Head of Kinsale, Friday, May 7, 1915, owing to the sinking of the Lusitania by torpedoes fired by a German submarine.

"We find that this appalling crime was committed contrary to international law and the conventions of all civilized nations.

"We also charge the officers of said submarine and the Emperor and Government of Germany, under whose orders they acted, with the crime of wholesale murder before the tribunal of the civilized world.

"We desire to express sincere condolences and sympathy with the relatives of the deceased, the Cunard Company and the United States, many of whose citizens perished in this murderous attack on an unarmed liner."

CAPTAIN TURNER'S TESTIMONY

Captain W. T. Turner, the Lusitania's commander, was the chief witness at the inquest.

The Coroner asked the captain whether he had received a message concerning the sinking of a ship off Kinsale by a submarine. Captain Turner replied that he had not.

Did you receive any special instructions as to the voyage?"

'Yes, sir."

Are you at liberty to tell us what they were?"

"No, sir."

"Did you carry them out?"

"Yes, to the best of my ability."

"You were aware threats had been made that the ship would be torpedoed?"

"We were," the captain replied.

"Was she armed?"

"No, sir."

"What precautions did you take?"

"We had all the boats swung when we came within the danger zone, between the passing of Fastnet and the time of the accident."

"Tell us in your own words what happened after passing Fastnet."

SAW THE TORPEDO

"The weather was clear' Captain Turner answered.

"We were going at a speed of eighteen knots. I was on the port side and heard Second Officer Hefford call out, 'Here's a torpedo.'

"I ran to the other side and saw clearly the wake of a torpedo. Smoke and steam came up between the last two funnels. There was a slight shock. Immediately after the first explosion there was another report, but that may possibly have been internal.

"I at once gave the order to lower the boats down to the rails, and I directed that women and children should get into them. I also had all the bulkheads closed.

"I also gave orders to stop the ship," Captain Turner continued, "but we could not stop. We found that the engines were out of commission. It was not safe to lower boats until the speed was off the vessel. As a matter of fact, there was a perceptible headway on her up to the time she went down.

"When she was struck she listed to starboard. I stood on the bridge when she sank, and the Lusitania went down under me. She floated about eighteen minutes after the torpedo struck her. My watch stopped at 2.36. I was picked up from among the wreckage and afterward was brought aboard a trawler.

"No warship was convoying us. I saw no warship, and none was reported to me as having been seen. At the time I was picked up I noticed bodies floating on the surface, but saw no living persons. "

Eighteen knots was not the normal speed of the Lusitania, was it?" he was asked.

"At ordinary times," answered Captain Turner, "she could make twenty-five knots, but in war times her speed was reduced to twenty-one knots. My reason for going eighteen knots was that I wanted to arrive at Liverpool without stopping and within two or three hours of high water."

DOUBLE LOOKOUTS ON LINER

"Was there a lookout kept for submarines, having regard to previous warnings?"

"Yes; we had double lookouts."

"Were you going a zigzag course at the moment the torpedoing took place?"

"No; it was bright weather, and land was clearly visible."

"Was it possible for a submarine to approach without being seen?"

"Oh yes, quite possible."

"Something has been said regarding the impossibility of launching the boats on the port side?"

"Yes," said Captain Turner, "owing to the listing of the ship."

"How many boats were launched safely?"

"I cannot say."

"Were your orders promptly carried out?"

"Yes."

"Was there any panic on board?"

"No, there was no panic at all; it was almost calm."

By the foreman of the jury:

"In the face of the warnings at New York that the Lusitania would be torpedoed, did you make any application to the Admiralty for an escort?"

"No, I left that to them. It is their business, not mine. I simply had to carry out my orders to go, and I would do it again."

Captain Turner uttered the last words of this reply with great emphasis.

By the coroner:

"I am very glad to hear you say so, Captain,"

By a juryman:

Did you get a wireless to steer your vessel in a northerly direction?"

"No," replied Captain Turner.

"Was the course of the vessel altered after the torpedoes struck her?"

"I headed straight for land, but it was useless.

Previous to this the water-tight bulkheads were closed.

I suppose the explosion forced them open. I don't know the exact extent to which the Lusitania was damaged."

"There must have been serious damage done to the water-tight bulkheads."

"There certainly was, without doubt."

"Were the passengers supplied with lifebelts?"

"Yes."

"Were any special orders given that morning that lifebelts be put on?"

"No."

NO WARNING GIVEN

"Was any warning given you before you were torpedoed?"

"None whatever. It was suddenly done and finished."

"If there had been a patrol boat aboard; might it have been of assistance?"

"It might, but it is one of those things one never knows."

With regard to the threats against his ship, Captain Turner said he saw nothing except what appeared in the New York papers the day before the Lusitania sailed. He never had heard the passengers talking about the threats, he said.

"Was a warning given to the lower decks after the ship had been struck?" Captain Turner was asked.

"All the passengers must have heard the explosion," Captain Turner replied.

Captain Turner in answer to another question said he received no report from the lookout before the torpedo struck the *Lusitania*.

OTHER TESTIMONY

Cornelius Horrigan, a waiter aboard the *Lusitania*, testified that it was impossible to launch boats on the starboard side because of the steamer's list. He went down with the ship, but came up and was rescued. Horrigan gave a partial identification of one of the bodies, which he thought to be that of Steward Cranston.

The ship's bugler, Vernon Livermore, gave evidence that the water-tight compartments were closed, but thought that the explosion must have opened them. No one was able to identify a man in whose pocket was found a card bearing the name of John Wanamaker of New York, and in the left-hand corner " Notary Public MacQuerrie, Bureau of Information."

CORONER HORGAN'S STATEMENT

Coroner Horgan said that the first torpedo fired by the German submarine did serious damage to the *Lusitania*, but that, not satisfied with this, the Germans had discharged another torpedo. The second torpedo, he said, must have been more deadly, because it went right through the ship, hastening the work of destruction.

He charged that the responsibility 'lay on the German government and the whole people of Germany who collaborated in the terrible crime. "This is a case," he said, "in which a powerful war- like engine attacked an unarmed vessel without warning

It was simple barbarism and cold-blooded murder.

"I purpose to ask the jury to return the only verdict possible for a self-respecting jury — that the men in charge of the German submarine were guilty of willful murder."

CHAPTER XXI Universal Condemnation

NOT EVEN the invasion of peaceful Belgium, or any of the other atrocities charged to the belligerent nations in the Great War, stirred such universal and emphatic condemnation as the destruction of the Lusitania and over half its human freight of human lives. From all quarters of the globe the cry of amazement, indignation and outrage arose.

One of the first to express his feelings was President Theodore Roosevelt, who said: **"This represents not merely piracy, but piracy on a vaster scale of murder than any old-time pirate ever practiced.**

"This is the warfare which destroyed Louvain and Dinant and hundreds of men, women and children in Belgium carried out to innocent men, women and children on the ocean and to our own fellow countrymen and countrywomen who are among the sufferers.

"It seems inconceivable that we should refrain from taking action in this matter, for we owe it not only to humanity, but to our own national self-respect."

Other Reactions

Atlee Pomerene, U. S. Senator from Ohio, member of the Foreign Relations Committee, said: "To Americans the sinking of the Lusitania is the most deplorable incident of the European war. Every man with the milk of human kindness in his breast condemns any policy by any nation that leads to the slaughter without warning of babes, women and non-combatants."

Morris Sheppard, U. S. Senator from Texas, said: "The sinking of the Lusitania is an illustration of the unspeakable horror of modern warfare, and will be a tremendous argument for general disarmament when the war closes. Let us handle the present situation with patience and calmness, trusting the President to take the proper course."

John W. Griggs, former Governor of New Jersey and at one time Attorney-General of the United States, expressed himself emphatically on the *Lusitania* tragedy. He said: "The time for watchful waiting has passed. No investigating committee is needed. The facts are known. Action is demanded. A demand should be made at once without waiting by the government to get the finding of any investigations or inquests. Would you hesitate to act if a man slapped you in the face? I do not say what should be demanded. That is for the government to decide.

But an explanation should be demanded of Germany at once. The German submarine violated a law that even savages would recognize. I would hold Germany to account by proclaiming her an outlaw among the nations of the world. If the German government pleads that it was justified in this crime — which it will — it is then the duty of the United States with other neutral nations to cut her off from the rest of the world."

The RMS Lusitania

Conclusion

This volume reviewed three major events in world history as described by the great author Logan Marshall. Number one we experienced the saga of the *Titanic*.

Passengers who stepped on to the giant ship were living in an era of peace and tranquility. The United States had not been at war for over a decade and the Spanish-American War was of short duration.

Marshall's account was the first to be published after the horrific tragedy and he managed to convey the factual data along with the verbiage to give readers a feeling that they were there. When the *Titanic* left Southampton the passengers were not aware that at the bottom of the ship hundreds of tons of blazing coal was smoldering against a one inch thick steel hull. The *Titanic* was a double bottomed ship, but did not have a double hull.

Marshall conveys all the excitement and splendor as the *Titanic* sailed away on her maiden voyage. Everything went perfectly until 11:40 am on April 14, 1912 when the Titanic slammed into an iceberg.

Most of the passengers were unaware of the event. It was not a traumatic encounter and the only sign was that there was soon no vibration coming from the engines. Captain Smith quickly learned that his ship was doomed.

If you read between the lines you realize that the Captain is dazed and not acting too rationally. Why did he launch his early lifeboats with so much vacant space? Unfortunately the people on board did not realize that the ship was doomed but Captain Smith did!

For many minutes after the *Titanic*'s encounter, passengers are laughing and joking about the unusual event.

Everyone on the *Titanic* could have been saved if they had just had enough lifeboats. *Titanic* was one of the few ships that sank in a way that the lifeboats on both the starboard and port sides could have been launched.

Marshall pointed out that the price to have enough safety craft for all the passengers was minimal but the lifeboats blocked the views from the cabins and the White Star Line would lose profits.

Titanic stayed afloat for two hours and forty minutes. The horrible tragedy was compounded because there were ships close by that could have possibly saved everyone. Fortunately the *Titanic* reached the *Carpathia* 58 miles away by wireless. Captain Rostron of the *Carpathia* rushed to the *Titanic*, but he arrived hours after the final plunge and too late to rescue the majority of the passengers.

Most historians today discount the importance of the coal fire on the *Titanic*. We're going to give you information from the 1912 British Hearings and let you the readers decide if the fire was significant in the demise of the great ship.

Here's testimony from day four of the British Hearings from lead fireman Frederick Barrett.
(Mr. Lewis - To the Witness.)
"Now, with regard to the bunker, you have said this bunker referred to just now was empty - the coal bunker?
- Yes.
2293. Were there any other coal bunkers empty forward?
- No.
2294. Was this the only one empty?
- Yes.

2295. Had it been emptied in the usual way?
- No.
2296. Why was it emptied?
- My orders were to get it out as soon as possible.
2297. When did you receive those orders?
- Not very long after the ship left Southampton.
2298. Was there anything wrong?
- Yes.
2299. What was wrong?
- The bunker was a-fire.
2300. Shortly after you left Southampton -
The Commissioner:
Now how is this relevant to this Inquiry?
2301. Shortly after you left Southampton - I'll put another question or two, and you will see why I think it is relevant. (To the Witness.) How long did it take them to work the coal out?
- Saturday.
2302. The whole Saturday. What condition was the watertight bulkhead in?
- It was the idea to get the bunker out. The chief engineer, Mr. Bell, gave me orders: "Builder's men wanted to inspect that bulkhead."
2303. The bulkhead forms the side of the bunker.
2304. What was the condition of the bulkhead running through the bunker?
- It was damaged from the bottom.
2305. Badly damaged?
- The bottom of the watertight compartment was dinged aft and the other part was dinged forward.
2306. (The Commissioner.) What do you attribute that to?
- The fire.
2307. Do you mean to say the firing of the coal would dinge the bulkhead?
- Yes.

2308. (Mr. Lewis.) This is the bulkhead between sections 5 and 6?
- Yes." (End of Barrett's testimony.)
Here we have to remember that the *Titanic* was constructed so that four of her front compartments could be compromised and the ship would still stay afloat. Once the 5th compartment was holding water it was just a matter of time until the ship sank.
Now let's review the testimony at the British Hearings of another survivor who was a fireman. His name was Charles Hendrickson and here's his 1912 testimony. ----
Charles Hedrickson British Inquiry Day 5 Questioned by Mr. Lewis--
5232. Do you remember a fire in a coal bunker on board this boat?
- Yes.
5233. Is it a common occurrence for fires to take place on boats?
- No.
5234. It is not common?
- No.
5235. How long have you been on a White Star boat?
- About five years.
5236. When did you last see a fire in a coal bunker?
- I never saw one before.
5237. It has been suggested that fires in coal bunkers are quite a common occurrence, but you have been five years in the White Star line and have not seen a fire in a coal bunker?
- No.
5238. Did you help to get the coal out?
- Yes.
5239. Did you hear when the fire commenced?
- Yes, I heard it commenced at Belfast.

5240. When did you start getting the coal out?
- The first watch we did from Southampton we started to get it out.
5241. How many days would that be after you left Belfast?
- I do not know when she left Belfast to the day.
5242. It would be two or three days, I suppose?
- I should say so.
5243. Did it take much time to get the fire down?
- It took us right up to the Saturday to get it out.
5244. How long did it take to put the fire itself out?
- The fire was not out much before all the coal was out.
5245. The fire was not extinguished until you got the whole of the coal out?
- No. I finished the bunker out myself, me and three or four men that were there. We worked everything out.
5246. The bulkhead forms part of the bunker - the side?
- Yes, you could see where the bulkhead had been red hot.
5247. You looked at the side after the coal had been taken out?
- Yes.
5248. What condition was it in?
- You could see where it had been red hot; all the paint and everything was off. It was dented a bit.
5249. It was damaged, at any rate?
- Yes, warped.
5250. Was much notice taken of it? Was any attempt made to do anything with it?
- I just brushed it off and got some black oil and rubbed over it.
5251. To give it its ordinary appearance?
- Yes.
5252. You are not a professional expert and would not be able to express an opinion as to whether that had any effect on the collision?
- I could not say that.

It is the opinion of the editors of this volume that the coal fire should not be ignored and most probably it played a major part in the ultimate sinking of the *Titanic.* Marshall's text does not include data from the hearings, but we praise his journalistic skills because he was the only 1912 author that wrote a book that discussed the fire in great detail. Years later the famous radio journalist Paul Harvey did a segment about the fire on the Titanic which he titled—"The Rest of the Story."

After the *Titanic* sank Marshall takes us from the best of political times into the worst of political times. An assassination in 1914 causes a major conflagration in Europe and Asia. In great detail he gives us a 1914 play by play description of the adversaries and why they reacted in the way they did.

We conclude our narrative with Marshall's brilliant account of what happened on the *Lusitania*. The *Lusitania* sank in 1915 and of the 1198 victims, over 100 were Americans.

As we read Marshall's account of the Titanic and Lusitania we realize that that there were major differences. Whereas the people on the Titanic initially considered the clash with the iceberg as a novelty, the passenger on the *Lusitania*—knew immediately that their ship was in major trouble. The *Titanic* sank in two hours and 40 minutes and the *Lusitania* sank in only 18 minutes.

Fortunately for the passengers of the *Lusitania* the water was much warmer than the area where the *Titanic* sank. As Marshall pointed out, passengers on the *Lusitania* survived after spending hours in the water. *Titanic* passengers with only their life jackets would stay conscious for only a few minutes.

Titanic survivors had no need to worry about warships in their midst. The worry that rescue vessels would be attacked near the *Lusitania* made the rescue efforts more difficult.

A bit of coincidence was that the *Lusitania* sank close to Queenstown Ireland which was the last city the *Titanic* visited prior to her demise.

Marshall's writings about the *Lusitania* came out in 1915. After the *Lusitania* sank for a long period the Germans did not harm ships from America. In 1917 they again began looking for civilian targets. Also in 1917 the United States intercepted a telegram from Germany called the "Zimmermann Telegram".

This message told Mexico that if they joined the war on Germany's side that Germany would see that Mexico got several of our states back after she won --- states like Texas!

Because of Germany's change in her behavior regarding passenger ships and the American reaction to the Zimmermann Telegram the United States entered the war in 1917.

It didn't take too long and the war was over! Our American "doughboys" could really fight!

The End

Books by Ken Rossignol

The Privateer Clause 1ST in the Series--- Cruising has never been more dangerous! This first in the series introduces Marsha and Danny Jones in a thriller that takes the *Sea Empress* through serious threats to every life on the ship!

RETURN OF THE SEA EMPRESS

2nd in the Series --- Would you want the President of the United States on your cruise ship? Find out what took place as the president joined the ship after the *Sea Empress* left Europe for Florida.

FOLLOW TITANIC

3rd in the Series - One hundred years after the *Titanic* went to its grave, excitement and adventure awaits those on the *Sea Empress* as the ship suddenly diverts to a northerly crossing of the Atlantic.

FOLLOW TRIANGLE – VANISH

4th in the Series --- Join Marsha & Danny Jones as they continue to secure the safety of the Sea Empress, now on its way to the Caribbean. Sen. Lyndon Langdon, the choice of the President to fill a coming vacancy on the Supreme Court is onboard. An expert is on the ship to discuss the history of the Bermuda Triangle. The Sea Empress arrives at St. Thomas to a remarkable discovery.

The original facts and details of the Titanic disaster from the newspapers of the world bring forward the story in a vivid and striking way!
Join the news stories in action as the first reports told of the RMS Titanic being towed to Halifax and all the passengers saved in erroneous first reports.
Learn how the survivors were saved and about the heroes of the night who sacrificed their own lives so that others may live.

TITANIC 1912 The story of the heroes and the wonderful new wireless device that was so critical in saving lives as well as

startling new details of a fire on board the Titanic which had been burning since the ship left port in Southampton. These details and others were on the front pages of great newspapers beginning hours after the ship sank. The U.S. Senate convened a hearing three days following the plunge to the ocean floor by the greatest ship ever built to that day.
Why did Capt. Smith ignore warnings of ice fields ahead?
Why were there only enough lifeboats for one-third of the passengers?
Was the ship speeding?
See the best photos and graphics that survive from the original coverage in this great book AND in the paperback version now available on Amazon.
This book also available on Kindle by a 21st century reporter looking back at the most significant disaster to that day in the 20th century will help you separate the facts from the fiction.
Rossignol also speaks on cruise ships around the world on the Titanic, the Bermuda Triangle and other maritime subjects.

The Chesapeake: Tales & Scales is the first in the series

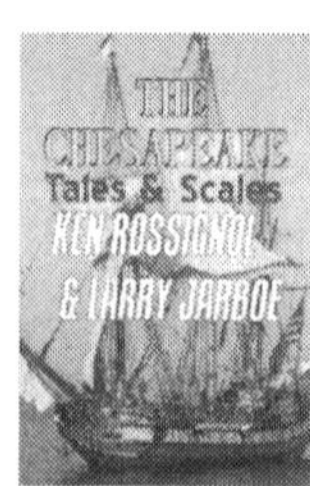

of short stories that have appeared in *The Chesapeake* over the years. Join Jack Rue, Pepper Langley, Mel Brokenshire, Cap'n Larry Jarboe, Ken Rossignol, Vi Englund, Frederick L. McCoy, Stephen G. Uhler, Alan V. Cecil and Alan Brylawski as we explore the land of the flask, the fiddle and the dark roasted possum!

The Chesapeake: Legends, Yarns, & Barnacles ---
The second in the series of short stories from the pages of *The Chesapeake*! Great fishing instructions wrapped in irony about sailing, boating and hunting. Littered with buzzards and lighthouses, the sagas of the tidewater region of the Chesapeake Bay and Southern Maryland will delight every reader!

The Story of THE RAG!

The true life story of the *St. Mary's Today* newspaper—the small-town newspaper that won a landmark First Amendment decision that went all the way to the Supreme Court when a sheriff, state's attorney, and a posse of deputies cleaned out newsstands to keep voters from reading critical articles before voting. The decision, Rossignol v. Voorhaar, was issued by the Fourth Circuit United States Court of Appeals. Now available as an ebook, and in paperback with loads of great editorial cartoons!

Books by Bruce Caplan

The Sinking of the Titanic

Now in its 18th printing in paperback, the 1912 original has been abridged and edited by the nationally known author Bruce M. Caplan. Caplan appears before audiences nationwide and lectures on cruise ships around the world on the Titanic disaster. The 100th Anniversary Commemorative edition is now in Kindle for the first time, due to popular demand!

Buster Boppington and his Talking Dog

"Buster Boppington and his talking dog Nappy embark on a rollercoaster ride of fantasy, excitement and mystery!"

13346307R00109

Made in the USA
Charleston, SC
02 July 2012